PROJECTS IN PROPERTY

The business of residential property development

Denis Minns, MSc FRICS

Published October 2023

ISBN 978-1-7391349-5-2

Bath Publishing Limited
27 Charmouth Road
Bath
BA1 3LJ

Tel: 01225 577810
email: info@bathpublishing.co.uk
www.bathpublishing.com

Bath Publishing is a company registered in England: 5209173
Registered Office: As above

CONTENTS

Acknowledgements

I have been fortunate to work with first class professionals over many years from whom I have gained my knowledge and experience. There are too many to name but I thank them all.

Foreword

It was 2009 and the effects of the financial crash were still being felt by development companies. Lending banks had changed their criteria and were keen to adjust their loans to comply with their more restricted terms. I recall one banker at NatWest informing me that my company 'just needed another £500,000 to balance the loan book'. On a buyer's market with sales difficult to achieve, where would we get £500,000 from? The answer came from an unexpected direction. Further funds had been agreed in principle to buy a new site subject to a secured lending valuation. Then disaster. The surveyor undertaking the valuation for the bank down-valued the site to such an extent that it was impossible for us to proceed with the loan. We were forced to sell on our purchase option.

And then luck and coincidence came by hand in hand – we sold that option on for a profit. The profit was exactly £500,000.

Introduction

I began writing these words at the start of isolation at home compelled by the 2020 coronavirus. It seemed at that early stage of the crisis that the economy, including financial markets and the property markets, would suffer a period of recession. Recessions are invariably followed by periods of expansion, and, given the factors of high demand for residential property, low interest rates, limited housing supply and the expansion of money supply, I felt that when the effects of the virus lessened we would see a significant growth in property prices. We did, but with interest rates now at much higher levels, demand has reduced though the markets remain resilient. This has much to do with the enduring nature of property and especially residential property in an economy that offers a limited supply.

This book is about residential development of property. Development is an active rather than a passive property play. It is one that has the social and economic benefits of bringing more homes into service to increase housing supply. New home and restoration projects feature innovation; renewable energy, creative design, high levels of insulation and broadband connectivity. The cost of maintenance is often low, making these homes more affordable to live in. I want to encourage and promote the success of residential develop-ment projects as not only are new homes a substantial benefit to our society, their development is speculation at its best, offering opportunities to create wealth for the developer.

An advantage in development of residential property that does not exist with property investment is perhaps obvious. Where an investment relies on income from the yield together with any growth in the property value over time, development offers the opportunity to create enhanced value by the design and construction of new homes or renovation of established buildings, that results from the development. That development is inspired by the developer who can gain a significant profit if they get it right and they know how to go about the process.

This book explains what is meant by property. It sets out strategies, advice, rules and suggestions to carry out residential development projects. It conducts the reader through the steps to be taken and compliance to be followed. It highlights pitfalls to be avoided and savings to be made. It takes the reader step by step through the acquisition, planning and project management process.

Residential property development is symbiotic with property law and the book explains this relationship. It highlights the laws of residential property development and the various legal requirements that shape the development process. Residential development projects are crafted from a complex fabric of land acquisition, planning, funding, building regulation, construction and sales. Within this fabric is woven many strands of property law that set out requirements, obligations and procedures that the developer or project manager needs to comply with in order to avoid potential pitfalls and to maximise returns.

Residential development offers great opportunities for wealth creation.

There is the opportunity to add value by new construction, rearranging the existing building or changing its use. Often these opportunities go side by side with difficulties and problems. I have identified problems that commonly arise and set out how these can be dealt with.

The book is more a work of reference than a page turner. I have presented the script with numbered separated headings so that the reader can use the book as a reference and more easily find subject headings and answers to questions on specific issues that arise throughout the development project.

Some templates which I use on a regular basis have been reproduced in the appendices. Those templates, along with others which are too difficult to reproduce in book form, are also included on an accompanying website, www. projectsinproperty.co.uk, in a format the reader can download and adjust.

Who am I?

I am a chartered surveyor with a particular interest in property law. I have been involved in every aspect of development with hundreds of residential development projects for over forty years. My experience has been with national housebuilding companies, specialist chartered surveyors and with small residential developers. My expertise and experience covers site acquisition, land use planning, project planning and construction, funding for residential development projects, and the selling and letting of new homes. For all these activities, property law is a common denominator and I hope this book explains the importance of property law and helps the developer identify the legal requirements of the residential development process and understand how these requirements affect projects.

Strategic land use planning is not part of this book. That is for the household name companies staffed by a range of professionals who need no guidance from me as to how to go about their business. Neither do I comment on the construction process itself save where decisions as to method and materials impact on the project's development.

I hope this book will help the developer identify and avoid the pitfalls of residential development and find answers to resolve them if they occur. I hope, too, that the book helps maximise the opportunities in residential development and to make profitable projects in property.

Who are you?

This book is directed at small scale developers and those wishing to become small scale developers. It is not directed at the national housebuilders. Many of these have all the resources of a public company and a whole range of expert staff to turn to. The national developers are well placed to provide the volume of homes our country needs. So why do we need small scale developers?

Small scale developers are defined as those who undertake small developments, both new builds and restoration projects. These developments are not of interest to national developers but they are more often sited in sustainable urban areas close to all the facilities and where there is strong and established demand. Potential development sites are often identified long before these sites become available for construction with small developers engaging in negotiations and often acquiring interests for site assembly.

Small development sites frequently require demolition of obsolete buildings or restoration of existing buildings – it is rare for such sites to consist of open fields. Individual homes (which could include bespoke houses for clients) are regularly designed to enhance an existing neighbourhood rather than designed from a standard plans book.

So why is it that the number of small developers active in the market is at an all-time low? As you read through this book you will begin to discover the answer to this question. It is my hope that this book will help to identify issues and provide solutions.

There is potentially a large number of small scale developers and those wishing to become involved in the industry. However, the complexities encountered by the small scale developer restrict the numbers willing to take the risk. If this book helps to de-mystify the process and assists the would-be developer in their quest, the country will benefit hugely from the creation of more new homes.

It is my aim to see more small scale developers profiting from projects in property.

Case studies

I have included some case studies below some chapters which I hope will contribute a practical understanding of the text. I have also included some 'mistakes' that I consider I have made over the years to demonstrate I do not always get things right. I hope the reader does not repeat the same mistake!

> *'Instead of learning from other people's success learn from their mistakes.'*
> Jack Ma

There is a lot to be said for learning from the mistakes of others. It is a lot better than making the mistakes oneself. The success or failure of residential development projects is dependent on many different circumstances. Often these circumstances are out of the developer's control and also often unknown and unexpected. In many cases one 'key issue' stands out as the problem that needed to be solved. Occasionally an issue arises that is completely unexpected. Perhaps the developer should not feel that they are always responsible for mistakes.

List of acronyms

Throughout the book I have used various acronyms which are listed here for information.

AI	Approved Inspector
AST	Assured Shorthold Tenancy
AVM	Automated Valuation Model
BNG	Biodiversity Net Gain
CBR	California Bearing Ratio
CDM	Construction Design Management
CGT	Capital Gains Tax
CIL	Community Infrastructure Levy
CIS	Construction Industry Scheme
CML	Council of Mortgage Lenders
CSA	Contract Sum Analysis
CWa/F	Collateral Warranty Funder
DCMS	Department for Culture, Media and Sport
EA	Environment Agency
EPC	Energy Performance Certificate
FRA	Flood Risk Assessment
FENSA	Fenestration Self Assessment Scheme
GDV	Gross Development Value
GPDO	General Permitted Development Order
GEA	Gross External Area
GIA	Gross Internal Area
HETAS	Heating Equipment Testing and Approvals Scheme
HoT	Heads of Terms
HMO	House in Multiple Occupation
HMRC	His Majesty's Revenue and Customs
HSE	Health & Safety Executive
IHT	Inheritance Tax
JCT	Joint Contracts Tribunal
JV	Joint Venture
LPA	Local Planning Authority
LTV	Loan To Value
MCS	Microgeneration Certificate Scheme
M&E	Mechanical and Electrical
NHBC	National House Builders Council
PAYE	Pay As You Earn
PI	Professional Indemnity
PMS	Project Monitoring Surveyor

PV   Photovoltaic
QS   Quantity Surveyor
RICS   Royal Institution of Chartered Surveyors
RLV   Residual Land Value
RP   Registered Provider
SAP   Standard Assessment Procedure
SDLT   Stamp Duty Land Tax
SME   Small/Medium Enterprise
SPC   Special Purpose Company
SPV   Special Purpose Vehicle
P&T   Purchasers and Tenants
TER   Target Emission Rate
TPO   Tree Preservation Order
UKF   UK Finance
UKPN   UK Power Networks
VAT   Value Added Tax

Chapter 1

What is property?

'Property is the mind, not the body, of land and buildings.'
Denis Minns

*'It is the rule of law that upholds private property and provides
the framework for enterprise.'*
Margaret Thatcher

A useful starting point in a book about property is to understand what property is. When we talk of property we are referring to real property – land and buildings; houses; flats; industrial, civic and commercial buildings; and rural land. This is widely understood to be what we regard as property. This is not quite correct, however. Real property is more accurately the legal rights, rules and responsibilities that attach to the ownership or occupation of land and buildings. Property is the intangible and invisible presence within a building or area of land that governs the scope of its use and its physical form. I call property 'The mind of land and buildings' because it is the mind that directs the functions, operations and limitations of the body.

Property derives from law, and property law is woven deep into the complex fabric of property development. This book exposes the strands of law woven into that fabric revealing many of the rules and requirements that the developer of property needs to observe and the opportunities that derive from the rule of law.

Indeed, property development takes place within a market economy that is enabled by the rule of law. It is the rule of law that regulates the requirements of property development, for example the identification of property by a formal postal address and the registration of ownership of land and the ability for third party interests, such as easements and covenants to be entered against property. Property is the source of security for debt and can be subject to a charge to the lender. Leases can be granted from property to allow exclusive possession subject to an annual payment of rent such that the casual observer is unaware of actual ownership. Utilities such as electricity, water and sewerage are available as of right to property owners with regulated charges and timescales for their connection. Ownership of property can be transferred from one legal person to another.

1

The rule of law extends to the enforcement of rights and responsibilities. Courts and tribunals exist for the jurisdiction and mediation of disputes and are readily accessible to claimants. Such law is generally available to all citizens and indeed this is often taken for granted. Taxes, levied on citizens and property, are fairly imposed to support the public realm. This rule of law derives from a social contract based on custom where the majority of citizens adhere to the law making it enforceable against those who do not.

To understand this we have to comprehend an economy where property does not exist in the form that we have it. There are, unfortunately, many economies in the world where this is the case – economies where the rule of law and particularly property law is absent or applies only to part of an economy. These are economies where there is no register of property and no proof of ownership so ownership is ascribed by occupation supported by collective local consent or else it is disputed; where there is no legal redress to claim debt or damages; where the transfer of interests is inhibited by an inability to prove ownership; where procedures for consents for development take years to obtain; where utilities are not available to all; and too often, where the absence of a universal social contract allows corruption to reside.

In his book *The Mystery of Capital*, Hernando de Soto reveals how economies without property and the rule of law have established capital in the shape of land and buildings. What they lack is the mechanism to use that capital in a way that creates wealth. His *Mystery of Capital* is his study of the factors that hold back economies from utilising capital assets to create wealth in the way that western economies do. His solution is clear – the application of a codified legal system that embraces 'extra legal' property, that's outside legal property law, subjecting it to a set of rules, regulations and principles applicable to all.

In an economy where the rule of law is in place, fairly accessed, generally understood and universally complied with, property law is the mechanism that allows assets to be activated to create wealth. This applies more to land and buildings than any other assets due to their permanence and value. Property law allows the rights of third parties to be registered as interests, such as easements, mortgage charges, restrictive covenants, public rights for services and leases. Limited liability companies can be formed to hold property subdividing shares among several investors and trusts can be formed in the names of several beneficiaries.

Margaret Thatcher said, '*The rule of law provides the framework for enterprise. It upholds private property and creates the market economy.*' The market economy is at the heart of the capitalist system and it is the capitalist system that creates wealth.

Residential property development is an enterprise that succeeds through capitalism.

Without the mind the human form is directionless and uncreative. Without property and where the rule of law is fractured or incomplete, land and buildings are dead capital. There, residential development is undertaken to provide shelter, and land is at best cultivated for crops but each lacks the vital mechanism to create wealth.

This is why we make the distinction between land and buildings and property.

It is to identify and capitalise on the opportunities that a system of property law offers us for the development of property and the opportunity to create wealth. To do so we need to observe those laws that regulate the development of property.

To appreciate the distinction between land and buildings and property, and to understand why I make it, let us take two identical buildings side by side. They are Romulus house and Remus house. They were both built by the same builder at the same time. They are the same design and the same specification. Each has a car park area to the rear.

Romulus house is owned freehold and occupied by an international company. It has exclusive use of the car park at the rear.

Remus house is let to various tenants on different leases with different terms and two of its floors are vacant. There are rights of access over part of the car park at the rear to neighbouring property.

These buildings are, as I have said, physically identical. They are not, however, identical properties. The rights and responsibilities of ownership are very different. Romulus house has a single owner and occupier while Remus house has a more fragmented arrangement of rights and responsibilities. This difference will impact on the value of the properties and value, which, as we will see later, is an integral feature of property.

Consider, too, when planning permission is granted for the demolition of an old house and the construction of a new block of flats. One could argue that the demolition of the old building takes away value as 'bricks and mortar' are to be taken away. It does not, of course. The developer perceives a greater value in the land given the planning permission granted than in the existing building. The right to build the new block of flats pursuant to the planning permission is the 'property right' that enhances value beyond the existing use value.

Value is one of the essential features of property. Property must be capable of having a value ascribed to it. That is not to say it is always valuable in terms of 'worth a lot of money'. Indeed, one might imagine that an area of land in the middle of a desert has very little value. If there is a remediation notice requiring the removal of polluted ground, for example, a property may have a negative value. What is important is that the property must be 'capable' of having a value ascribed to it. That valuation can only be supported by the certainty that derives from a codified and enforceable property law.

The second essential feature of property is one we have touched on – that of ownership. In order to transact property, whether by grant of rights, mortgages, leases or the sale of property, we must identify an undisputed owner. Two features serve this purpose – first, the identification of the property by official address; and second the registration of property. This is especially the case in England since 1990 when the register became open to inspection by the public.

When real property is sold it is not physically passed to the buyer as is chattel or personal property. A written contract is drawn up setting out the terms of sale and upon completion the new buyer is able to occupy the building on the terms agreed following legal completion and the signing of a transfer deed. Here is the third feature of property: it must be capable of being transferred from one party to another. That is not to say that the transfer of property cannot be restricted by contracts. Property must, however, be 'capable' of transfer.

Value, ownership and transferability are attributes of property that are incorporeal concepts rather than physical assets. They are the mind of land and buildings but in every sense we consider them part of the building – so why do we make this distinction between 'buildings' and 'property'? Does it really matter?

There are aspects of the property, that can be 'developed' without physical or operational development taking place. This development might be by variation of rights, surrender of a lease, change of use, enfranchisement and other legal actions affecting the property, not physical actions affecting the building. These are often the very actions that create enhanced value. We can see this by some simple examples.

A occupies a small flat in a residential block. The lease is subject to a restriction on sub-letting. **A** is planning to spend some time abroad and wishes to let his flat. He negotiates an amendment to the lease to allow him to do so. No physical development has taken place but he has enhanced its value.

B has a lease of 40 years on a flat in a smart London suburb. She negotiates a deal to extend the lease to 125 years. While she has had to pay the freeholder for the extension, the amount she pays is less than the amount by which she has enhanced the value of the flat.

C owns a dilapidated bungalow on a large plot. He obtains planning permission for re-development for 9 flats. The site for 9 flats with planning permission is worth more than the existing bungalow.

D owns a house with great potential to extend but subject to a restrictive covenant limiting any extension to the building. She obtains an order from the Upper Tribunal Lands Chamber for modification of the covenant thereby allowing her to extend the house and increase its value.

In all these cases **A**, **B**, **C** and **D** have enhanced the value of property without any physical activity to the building, but by a legal action that changes the 'property'.

Land and buildings within a state governed by the rule of law all have imbedded in them this vital mind that we call property. One cannot simply view a building to ascribe a value to it. One must understand the underlying 'property'. It may be subject to all kinds of limitations and onerous responsibilities. It may benefit from rights, or have some potential that would challenge an initial assumption of value. The developer must have the ability to interpret the property rights and responsibilities imbued within the building. They must distinguish property from land and buildings. They must be able to realise the opportunities that are offered by an understanding of the mind as well as the body of land and buildings.

Chapter 2

The property mantra

'SIR ANTHONY HABBERTON, Justice and Knight
Was enfeoffed of two acres of land
And it doesn't sound much till you hear that that site
Was a strip to the South of the Strand.'
Hilaire Belloc

2.1   Location, Location, Location

We have all heard the property mantra, but it seems to imply that location is the only thing that matters in property. Yes, location is important. A strip of 2 acres to the south of the Strand may indeed be a location of great value.

We have to acknowledge the importance of the location of property.

Residential property can be worth so much more when located in a private park rather than by a busy road out of town. Location might offer the convenience of being close to a town centre. It might offer peace away from main traffic routes. It may offer status of address or simply a pleasant neighbourhood. What we know with certainty is that the right location will always command the best price and a quick sale.

Location is, however, not the only attribute of property that contributes to its value. A more accurate mantra, though one less poetic, might be 'Location, Finance, Timing'.

2.2   The role of finance in property

Property will always have a value ascribed to it and often this value makes it expensive. The price will often be out of the reach of the resources of many buyers. Developers will often need to borrow money to buy property. We have seen the mechanisms that the rule of law imposes on the market economy and how property assets are used to obtain credit through a system of rules and regulations that allow property owners to secure credit. While the cost of finance may be seen as an influence on the price of property it is often the availability of finance which is the factor that contributes to the price of property. Developers will not necessarily be deterred when the cost of finance is high with substantial fees and high interest rates if they perceive the ability to earn greater returns due to rising values. What will always constrain borrowing, and thereby the price of property, is the availability of finance.

The availability of finance for development cannot be taken for granted though curiously it often is. There are several reasons why finance may be in short supply. If there is a downturn in property markets, banks will react swiftly.

Finance for property purchase is lent by way of a mortgage secured on the value of the property through a first charge to the lender registered on the title. It would be rare for a lender to lend the full value of the property and thereby a buffer is there so that if the value falls the owner may lose their stake but the bank is secure. Banks often lend between 50% and 70% loan to the value of the property. This is referred to as Loan To Value (LTV).

Some banks are limiting LTV for development finance to 60% due to uncertainty as to values and one major clearing bank has limited LTV to 45%. The old saying 'There is nothing as yellow as money' refers to the fear of losing money that will have investors and banks fleeing. Another obvious reason for the lack of availability of finance may be the security of an alternative investment with more reliable returns. Those with their own funds will have the ability to seek alternative investments such as shares rather than risk them on speculative development and banks will be no different. So the developer cannot assume that funders will rush to lend them finance.

A development loan is calculated as a percentage of the Gross Development Value of the project. We will see later in Chapter 11 what this means. The construction costs, fees and interest are deducted from the gross loan to be advanced as the project progresses, and the balance of the loan is then committed to the acquisition cost. This means that the developer commits their contribution upon legal completion of the purchase of the site.

Collateral security is, as the name suggests, property that is independent of the project upon which security can be offered to the lender. This is more often the case where there is some uncertainty as to the security being offered by the project itself or simply because the developer is requiring a higher LTV.

Where a potential site has no immediate development potential the developer will be well advised to seek an initial yield from the property. It almost does not matter what initial yield is being received but what is clear is that, after a protracted period awaiting the grant of planning permission and other consents, it will be satisfying to reflect that at least some income was being earned. It is preferable to buy a goose that lays eggs while it is being fattened up for Christmas. With property it is possible to acquire both the income and the enhancement.

For example, if a property is acquired for access to a future development site where negotiations are to take place with further landowners, the developer should be sure to let it rather than have it stand vacant.

Many successful property deals have been done by operational companies that occupy a property for their own trading thereby not having to let it. They seek change of use or some form of development while in occupation and capitalise on an increase in value after a period of occupation. Companies such as Ikea and McDonalds occupy property for their operations, building substantial portfolios. Many others acquire property for commercial use with the future intention of development. Speculation is thereby mitigated by their use of the property while redevelopment plans are in process.

Interest rates are a key factor in housing demand. Low interest rates, however, do not mean that buyers will necessarily buy property. The famous economist JK Galbraith points out that the assumption that people will 'always speculate if only they can get the money to finance it could not be further from the truth. There have been many periods of plentiful and cheap finance when speculation was negligible.' What motivates buyers then is the perception that values will rise, not the cost or availability of finance.

In theory a development project purchased wisely has the inbuilt ability for value enhancement as the implementation of the development will, with skilled project management, result in increased value upon completion.

2.3   The timing of transactions in property

Property markets move in cycles. These cycles travel through periods technically termed recovery, expansion, hyper-supply and recession. And that means the timing of transactions can make a great deal of difference to the supply and demand and thus to price. We have all heard the terms 'Buyers' market' and 'Sellers' market.' When demand from buyers is high, prices rise and when demand is low prices can fall. When the market is bust then this creates a buyers' market and when the market is booming this creates a sellers' market.

This cycle works as a period of rise, recovery and expansion to which supply increases causing over supply and thus recession. This is one thing we can be sure of with property markets. A boom is followed by a bust just as sure as a bust will be followed by a boom. What we will never know, however, is when the demand will change, and what the effect will be of the change.

One may recognise the cycle. It is as in Genesis 41. Seven years of abundance followed by seven years of famine. Something to do with Joseph counting cattle. With property markets this period is often estimated to be approximately 16 to 18 years.

When we look at recent residential property cycles we see that the peaks have been 1973, 1989 and 2006. By simple calculation we should have anticipated the peak in the housing market around 2022. We have to add two significant factors, however.

First, there can be 'troughs' in periods when markets were rising when it feels like a fall is coming but it does not last for long. This can manifest as a stagnant market. In a stagnant market, sellers keen to sell will inevitably have to reduce prices which to some may appear like a buyers' market but strictly speaking it is not a bust. The bust follows the boom. Also, inevitably, there will be circumstances at a micro level that create demand and therefore increases in prices in a particular area during a bust market. Again this can lead observers to believe that the market is rising.

So is the time to buy property during the rising years not the falling years? I think not. A buyer may well secure a bargain when prices are falling and there is a greater inventory to choose from. Residential development projects are always more likely to have a successful outcome when bought at a reasonable price. Over-paying for a site will invariably lead to difficulties and the developer must carefully analyse the financial implications and viability of the project to ensure that they are not over-paying.

Residential development projects take time to acquire, to achieve planning permission, to construct and to sell. If the whole process will take two years, it may be that an ideal time to buy a project is in a stagnant market two years prior to an anticipated boom such that sales can take place as the market rises. In practice it is rarely possible to get the timing just right but it is always well worth keeping an eye on the factors that drive the market. This applies equally when holding houses for sale prior to the market changing to bust. I recall a major and well respected residential development company putting five new houses on the market in November 1988 prior to intending to commence construction in 1989. This was generally seen locally as defeatist as surely prices would rise in the New Year? The company managed to secure sales on two of the houses with three being sold one year later. The two houses sold before the market fell achieved nearly £100,000 more than those sold one year later. I myself once sold two houses off plan at £390,000 each. One year later the very same house types on the rest of the estate were sold for £350,000 each. An astute move by the developer and, in my case I admit, pure good fortune but in each case an illustration of the importance of timing.

In addition to the cycle there are other factors of timing that drive residential property markets. These can be macro issues, for example, issues affecting national markets like a fall in the value of the pound which might stimulate foreign buyers who hold currencies that buy more pounds. Political uncertainty following an election with no clear winner will also tend to suppress all asset markets.

At a local level, supply of similar homes may soak up the buyers, poor broadband connection will discourage buyers, the discontinuation of a bus route could affect a project of housing for the elderly. The announcement of a new Waitrose store may raise the status of an area and house prices in it. These are all factors that may affect the value of new homes but there are perhaps two factors that are always present and will always affect markets.

Firstly, property markets are affected by finance markets. A fall in stock prices will generally cause investors to become nervous about housing markets. This may take some time to ricochet from stocks to residential property. I recall the stock market crash in October 1987 did not affect house prices until the beginning of 1989. It was not a crash that followed but a tortuous decline in values as markets adjusted a mini boom in house prices the previous year and a crash in stock markets with reductions in credit affecting housing markets.

Secondly, Government policy also affects housing markets. The impact of Government policy can determine demand in housing markets and taxation is often the cause of this. Property taxes may make investment in residential property less attractive and conversely, reduction in taxation will stimulate demand for houses. The 'holiday' from stamp duty land tax is an example of this where buyers rushed to complete on purchases prior to expiry of the holiday in June 2021.

Perhaps nothing could more seriously affect property markets than a global pandemic. Mercifully, such pandemics are a rare occurrence and my own view is that now that the effects of the pandemic are past, residential property will continue to rise in value given money creation, inflation and rise in asset prices that will follow.

The developer is therefore subject to an economic cycle and susceptible to a number of additional factors that can disrupt both supply and demand. Residential development is a speculative undertaking without guarantees. It involves substantial risk and requires vision, caution, patience, understanding and at least some expertise.

Chapter 3

The business of residential property development

'I dream my painting and then I paint my dream.'
Vincent van Gough

Residential property development is a business undertaken for profit. We have seen that where property is not an element in the development, what results is merely a construction activity that creates shelter. There is no ability to create wealth as the legal framework we call property is absent. We are fortunate to live in a country that has a well established property law that underpins development as a business – the incorporation of a limited liability company, the identification of ownership of property and the guarantee of ownership through the registration of title, the availability of consents and approvals to development plans and structures that endorse legitimacy and compliance that provide an assurance to buyers. These are ingredients that create value and value is essential to wealth and the business of residential property development.

3.1   The property developer

The developer is the proprietor of the residential development project. They must have the vision to see how property can be transformed from its existing use to a new and more profitable use. This vision is described in the quotation from van Gough. The developer must have a clear picture of the development in their mind before embarking on the project. They are the professional who oversees all aspects of the development to meet that vision. They need to believe that it can be done and have faith they can achieve it. Never doubting it. Never willing to concede defeat.

They need to understand a great many factors to be able to organise a residential development project. First, there is the acquisition of the site, ensuring that there is nothing to prevent the project from taking place. The property developer will need to ensure that planning permissions are in place and that all conditions to the planning permission are satisfied. They will need to appoint a team of professionals for the project ensuring that all are qualified and experienced in advising on the development they are to undertake. They must organise the construction works either by appointing a main contractor or subcontractors for specialist areas of the works. The developer's skills may be tested on matters such as taxation, company formation and insurance.

They will need to understand legal matters and their implications and of course they must be confident of the sale of the completed development.

I have referred to the developer as an individual. Perhaps more often the developer will be a company comprising several decision makers all with different areas of expertise. Alternatively, the developer may rely on a development team of professional consultants. Whatever the approach it is essential to 'dream the painting' and then to 'paint the dream'.

3.2   The development team
No developer will work alone on a residential development project. It is teamwork. The developer will appoint a team of professionals to work with them which will include an architect, engineers, surveyors and often many others. They will appoint subcontractors or a main contractor to carry out construction works and liaise with officers at the local planning and highway authority. Neighbourhood groups and special interest organisations will wish to review the proposals and these will often make useful contributions. The developer will need to arrange development finance and will therefore need the ability to work with people by coordinating, providing and presenting information about the project and motivating the team to share their vision to avoid delays and misunderstandings.

3.3   Setting up a residential development projects business
It was Walt Disney who said, '*The way to get started is to quit talking and start doing.*' This is good advice but it is worth the developer pausing to consider what type of business they are going to start. They will need to decide which of two methods to adopt. Will the business be a pure developer, or will it be a developer constructor? Simply, will it be engaging a main contractor to undertake all the works, or will it be undertaking the construction process itself supported by separate specialist subcontractors?

This decision may well depend on experience. The developer may not wish to project manage the construction process if they have no building experience or perhaps they wish to devote their energy to the acquisition of further projects. Conversely, if the developer has expertise in building they may wish to devote their energies to the construction process.

For a small developer there are advantages in project managing the construction process. The developer may be limited to one project which might give more time to concentrate on it. Funding several development projects is not easy and concentrating on just one project limits financial exposure. Dealing with subcontractors direct will also give insight as to costs such that the developer will learn how to put together budgets for residential development projects. There will no doubt be a saving in costs when undertaking construction project management rather than appointing a main contractor.

If the developer is looking to appoint a main contractor to handle all the works this will certainly free them up from the day-to-day construction process. They will need to enter into a building contract with the contractor setting out exactly what each party is responsible for. They will also wish to check the progress of the works as they proceed or they may wish to appoint a surveyor to undertake this on their behalf. The developer will be responsible for payments to the main contractor who will themselves settle the subcontractor accounts. This will usually be on a monthly basis. The clear advantage is that this arrangement has just one contractor to deal with, and the engagement of subcontractors is undertaken by the main contractor. This will, of course, come at a cost which could reduce the opportunity for the developer to maximise their return on the project.

3.4   Equipping the office

Let us consider what equipment is needed in order to operate a residential development project management business office. I say 'office' but I am not sure that an actual office is necessary to work from. Today we all have laptop computers which can be used just about anywhere so the expense of an office is probably unnecessary. If a developer does not have room at home they can consider working from a cabin on site or share an office.

Clearly, any business will need broadband connection. So much business is now done by email but more to the point a development business will require numerous documents and plans to be transmitted to consultants, bankers, lawyers and subcontractors as attachments to emails or through a document sharing app.

The ability to type documents, prepare spreadsheets and store data will be supplemented by a scanner, a printer and copier. Often one piece of equipment will achieve all of these functions and can usually be purchased quite cheaply.

Storing data on some sort of cloud facility will be an enormous advantage as the developer will be collating a large number of documents on a daily basis and the cloud offers an ideal storage system for this. It is important to file information in a logical way so that it can be retrieved easily.

The object is to create a logical and clearly understood filing system where colleagues can access documents if need be and that can be clipped as attachments to emails. When I receive documents that have someone else's reference I am sure to rename them for better identification before filing so that I can retrieve them easily.

There will need to be some kind of system to record all invoices. I code and collate all mine so that I can create an application for drawdown of development funds at the end of each month to send to my funding bank. It is also a useful record to access for VAT returns, CIS and accounts.

There is no need for printed letterheads. These can be created by a macro or image on a computer and selected each time a letter or email is sent. No need either for an expensive and space consuming plans and technical drawings printer. I email plans to my local print shop for collection when I am next passing. No need for a secretary. My communications are more usually by email.

I have someone to keep on top of my invoices, applications, bookkeeping and VAT and CIS returns. Many small accountants offer such services but I find a part-time employee preferable and I am fortunate to have such a good one.

3.5 Companies and partnerships
Limited liability companies

A great deal of business is conducted by limited liability companies. A limited liability company is an independent legal entity. The idea of a limited liability company is to limit liability for debts incurred by the company to the company's shareholdings and not its directors. This will mean that if the company becomes insolvent the directors will not be liable for its debts and the shareholders will lose only what they invested in the company.

This will be effective for those debts that are unsecured by way of charge on development sites. However, funders lending for development will usually require security by way of first charge on the development site and personal guarantees from the directors of the borrowing company. So too will any lenders of mezzanine finance though this will usually be secured by way of second charge behind the senior debt. So the owners of a limited liability development company are not in practice free from all liability if the company goes into liquidation.

The limited liability company will file annual accounts with Companies House and it should be noted that Companies House is increasingly keen to see filing in a timely manner.

The accounts will show the company's worth by way of a balance on the balance sheet incorporated in the accounts made up of accrued profit and shares. It is useful for a company to be able to demonstrate sustained profit in accounts as this will give credibility to the business. Corporation tax will be payable on the profit shown in the accounts following the end of the company's accounting year.

I consider the company to be the best vehicle for property development and indeed the developer who is to borrow from a specialist property lender to fund their development would be well advised to undertake the development under a limited company.

Limited Liability Partnerships (LLPs)
Partnerships do not have limited liability. The majority of partnerships are indeed general partnerships without limited liability. Liability for loss, misfeasance or damages is that of the partners jointly and severally. In the 1990s a series of legal proceedings were taken against large accountancy partnerships for damages where accounts were subsequently proven inaccurate. Such damages were often well beyond the professional indemnity insurance levels of these partnerships. Partners were potentially to be made bankrupt often for acts of others within the organisation of which they knew nothing. Following this, limited liability partnerships were created under the Limited Liability Partnership Act 2000 to allow the partnership entity to limit liability and thereby avoid partners potentially becoming bankrupt.

Special Purpose Vehicles (SPVs)
Sometimes called special purpose companies, SPVs are set up with the intention of carrying out a specific project, perhaps with the intention of closing down the SPV when the project is complete. The advantage of the SPV is that it carries no liabilities over from previous jobs and is often a favoured entity of lending banks. It is also a useful method of separating projects and there are thereby particular advantages to SPVs for residential development projects.

A separate bank account can be set up to receive drawdowns from a funder or joint venture partner and payments can be made from this account to contractors for construction works. Accounts can be simplified with such an arrangement as all transactions will be recorded on bank statements. There is no reason why a development organisation cannot brand SPVs similarly, for example, Blackbrook Project One Ltd, Blackbrook Project Two Ltd etc. The SPV is also a useful way of dealing with Joint Venture (JV) partners or investors who are concerned with one project only and have no interest in others. JV partners can be allocated shares in the SPV or make a loan to the SPV secured by way of second charge behind the project's lending bank.

If a developer is undertaking new construction work itself rather than employing a contractor then it will need to register the SPV for VAT, HMRC and the new homes warrantor. A better arrangement might be to set up a dedicated construction company to contract with all SPVs. In this way VAT, new home warranties and HMRC registrations can be continuous to a succession of projects. So, Blackbrook Construction Ltd undertakes work for Blackbrook Project One, Blackbrook Project Two etc and carries separate bank accounts for these projects to ensure that each project is ring fenced. JV partners and investors would be able to monitor the project simply from statements of the dedicated bank account should they wish. VAT is dealt with by Blackbrook Construction Ltd thus saving the project JV companies from having to register for VAT.

3.6   VAT
A residential development company will build new homes for sale. New homes built for sale are not exempt from VAT – they are zero-rated. This means that a construction company will claim back the VAT paid on its supplier's invoices on a monthly basis. Not all subcontractors will charge VAT on their invoices where they are aware that the project is a zero-rated new build. There are items that are standard-rated which include garden ornaments, white goods and ornamental landscaping.

If the project involves the refurbishment of an existing home then VAT will be charged. There can be reduced rates for some forms of conversions from commercial to residential use.

3.7   Payments to suppliers
Credit accounts with suppliers are a useful way of suspending payment for supplies usually on a monthly basis. I advise being realistic about the amount of credit required from a supplier. The developer should consider the cost of goods expected to be ordered from the supplier and not be tempted to use the supplier as a lending bank. The convenience of ordering goods for

delivery to site without up front payment is the purpose of a trade account, not securing maximum credit facilities.

Company vehicles are an expense to the business but an essential one. These can be owned by the business, or owned privately and charged to the business for fuel and wear and tear. There is a reasonable tax-free level available to those who use a personal vehicle for business and I consider private owner-ship, with a monthly expense payment made to the car owner for business mileage, to be the better option.

3.8   Staff

My organisation employs its staff in the construction company, not the development company, as it is the construction company that undertakes much of the day-to-day business.

The construction industry has often been criticised for engaging staff on a self-employed basis rather than taking on full time staff members. This has the advantage to the contractor of paying a gross amount without deduction of tax and avoiding deduction of national insurance. It is an industry that continually hires the services of bona fide subcontractors and it is no doubt tempting to extend the subcontractor status to personnel who are strictly staff. I have seen this particularly with site managers working on site who are engaged as independent contractors rather than employees. The Supreme Court held in the case of *Pimlico Plumbers Ltd v Smith* [2018] UKSC 29 that, notwithstanding Smith's engagement as a subcontractor, he was an employee and enjoyed rights under the Employment Rights Act 1996.

The main disadvantages to an 'employee' when working under the guise of a subcontractor are that there is no entitlement to holiday or sick pay and there will be greater difficulty in them obtaining a mortgage. There are, however, potentially greater risks. Subcontractors should consider that, as a subcontractor, they may be liable for pecuniary loss if they are managing a project that loses money where a lending bank insinuates that the loss is due to poor workmanship and it cannot obtain damages from the developer itself. A heavy price to pay for any subcontractor. My advice is certainly that a contractor employing site managers on construction sites should do so by way of an employment contract and certainly my advice to an 'employee' is to ensure that they are employed under an employment contract.

I once conducted an audit of staff to establish who were employed and who were self-employed using HMRC's rules of supervision, substitution, responsibility and the ability to work for others. My accountant came up with a simpler test. 'Who do you invite to the Christmas party?' he asked. His test corresponded exactly with my audit.

3.9   Cashflow

The developer must consider carefully the structure of the business before they begin trading. They should aim to run a business with a minimal general overhead and identify cashflow. Residential development projects generally take months to complete and it will not be sufficient to rely on profit at the completion of the project. Any business must regard cash as the 'oil in the engine'. Without the oil the engine will seize up. I factor in a project management fee charged by the construction company to the SPV and included in the bank's construction loan to cover outgoings on a monthly basis.

The business will benefit from the preparation of a cashflow forecast showing income and expenditure over a twelve month period. The starting point to such a cashflow forecast will be an analysis of expenditure to which will be added income from drawdowns and sales. One should always be realistic about expenditure and be sure to list everything – it is surprising how much can be spent each month and by listing everything it is possible to identify unnecessary expenditure. A cashflow statement is not a profit projection but a statement of cash in and out over a set period.

A tip from Richard Branson is to study the downside of a project before it is taken on. What might go wrong? What will be the overall effect on the business if it does? 'Always have the big picture at the forefront of your mind' is a useful piece of advice for the property developer as that big picture is the completed development sold to happy buyers.

3.10   People in property

Development of property is just one activity that takes place in property. It is perhaps worth considering some of the other activities requiring specialists to give an understanding how these may relate to a development project.

Estate agents

The estate agent is principally instructed to find buyers for the completed project. Many estate agents are involved in site assembly and acquisition. Commercial property agents tend to specialise rather than becoming involved in the sale of residential property.

Property management and letting agents

Prior to 1989 property management involved the management of blocks of flats in urban areas. This used to be seen as a rather dull activity consisting of organising schedules of inspection and repair, and collecting service charges for payment. Today property management incorporates residential property lets which not only adds vigour but can be a very profitable activity.

Property investors

Property is an asset class that has always been attractive to investors seeking a return not only from rents received but increases in the value of the property. Short term investment may be less attractive given higher rates of Stamp Duty Land Tax (SDLT) that now apply.

Valuers

Valuers are almost exclusively chartered surveyors. Valuations of property can be for compulsory purchase, leasehold enfranchisement, rating, taxation and numerous other matters as well as development.

Property lawyers

Most law firms have a specialist property department that deals with transactions and disputes in property. They are an important part of the process of the effective transfer and registration of property.

Dispute specialists

Disputes can be dealt with by lawyers but often a mediator will take this role. Mediation generally saves time and cost.

Land agents

There are still a great number of landed estates in our country. The old idea was that an estate manager would live on the estate and undertake the management of it. Today, firms of land agents fulfil this role.

Auctioneers

The attraction of an auction is something I consider later in this book. An auction can offer opportunities to a developer and certainly can be an effective way of selling surplus parcels of land.

Boundary surveyors

When a dispute arises with a neighbour regarding a boundary, a chartered surveyor will be appointed to resolve it. The disputed area is often a small piece of land but if it is part of the frontage to a development site it can be an important area of land despite its small size.

Architects
A project in property will need to be designed. A good architect is an essential requirement. They give advice, create planning drawings and prepare working drawings.

Planners
Planners used to be employed almost exclusively by Local Planning Authorities. Today many planners work in private practice. They assist the developer in putting together complex planning applications and advising on the likelihood of success of applications.

Engineers
The development project can often require the services of both structural and civil engineers.

All these roles are discussed later.

Chapter 4

Finding and acquiring a development project

'Such is the genius of capitalism that where a real demand exists
it does not go long unfilled.'
JK Galbraith

You may always be sure that the development project you have identified
has been identified by someone else before. It is a common feature of human
nature, however, that notwithstanding the ability of many to conceive an
idea, it is the ambition only of the few to implement it. That is to say that
many concepts, identified with vision, reasoned and formulated with great
accuracy, nevertheless require effort, risk, expertise, time and money to fulfill
them. Opportunity, it is said, often comes in overalls. The acquisition and
implementation of a development project is no exception.

4.1   The development project
So what is a development project? I suspect it is a little easier to identify than
describe. First, we should not be tricked into believing that a development
project depends on physical obsolescence of existing buildings. It is the
value of the existing buildings not their condition that is relevant. Physical
obsolescence is very likely the factor that gives the opportunity for development but economic obsolescence is also often the reason why a building
offers a development opportunity. Where the potential development value
of the site is higher than the current use value of the site, then there is a
development opportunity.

Planning permissions should be available for the development of the project.
This can be for a change of use of a building or operational development
such as demolition and new construction. The planning permission should
be either existing when a purchase is made or perceived to be obtainable
where perhaps the project is to be acquired conditional upon grant of the
required planning permissions or where the developer is prepared to take a
risk that it will be granted.

4.2   Development
Section 55(1) of the Town and Country Planning Act 1990 gives us the definition of development:

> *'The carrying out of building, engineering, mining or other opera-*
> *tions in, on, over or under land or the making of any material*
> *change in the use of any buildings or other land.'*

Development can, and often does, take the form of several different but related activities. Most often the project involves new construction work or perhaps refurbishment pursuant to some form of planning permission. This is in planning terms operational development defined in the section. That is to say, a form of development that alters the physical form of a building or land. This might include what we could describe as a 'make over', the updating of an existing house by, for example, stripping out an outdated kitchen and bathrooms, creating more open plan design and redecoration, sometimes incorporating limited construction works, right through to a huge city riverside apartments development in several large high rise blocks.

We have defined 'property' as something related to but distinct from construction. We should consider, too, property development that does not require construction but that nevertheless has the potential to increase in value.

4.3 Change of use
Section 55 (1) of the Town and Country Planning Act 1990 refers to material change of use as development.

As markets move, there become opportunities to change the use of a building to capitalise on the greater demand existing in an alternative use. Recently this emphasis has been on the change of use of old office, industrial and warehouse buildings into residential. Such change of use has always required planning permission but more recently changes in planning rules have allowed change of use in certain categories to take place under permitted development and thereby not requiring fresh planning permission.

Let us now look at some of the opportunities there might be to profit from a change of use of property and what might be involved in securing that change of use.

4.4 Permitted development
Section 57(1) Town and Country Planning Act 1990 states that planning permission is required for the carrying out of any development of land. You sometimes hear people say that permitted development does not require planning permission. However, technically it does. It is just that it does not require express permission. It will already have been permitted. Permission

will have been granted by a development order either general, local or by a special provision. Permitted development in the context of residential development would not have featured in a book such as this years ago save perhaps to point out that many planning permissions contain conditions that withdraw some classes of permitted development. Permitted development back then merely related to minor development.

Today it has a significant role following the Town and Country Planning (General Permitted Development) England Order 2015, Schedule 2 (from now on referred to as the GPDO) and the changes made to use classes in 2020.

This is principally due to the ability of developers to change the use of business accommodation to residential without planning permission under revised permitted development rules. This has had a profound effect on the availability of flatted development. The London Borough of Croydon heads the list of boroughs in London where office blocks have been altered to residential. The borough had a large number of redundant offices and the ability to change this use to residential has been beneficial both to owners of what were B1 buildings and to those seeking homes in the borough.

Use Classes are categorised. For example, Class O is office to residential, Class P is warehouse to residential and Class Q permitted development allows a change of use from agricultural to residential and the associated operations reasonably necessary to convert an agricultural building to a residential one. Class Q assumes the building is capable of functioning as a dwelling. The building must have the structural integrity to cope with the works. In other words, new structural work does not qualify. If extensive rebuilding is required, then that is a case for full planning permission, not permitted development (see *Hibbitt v SSCLG* [2016] EWHC 2853 (Admin)).

Use class categories have changed to offer significant opportunities to developers wishing to change the use of commercial property. These opportunities do not apply, however, in areas protected by planning restrictions such as Areas of Outstanding Natural Beauty and may indeed be subject to various limitations. A close examination of the circumstances relating to the property and its location is advised.

The grant of planning permission does not always create value. I think it was Lord Denning who once said, 'It is planning permission coupled with demand that creates value'. It is quite possible to obtain planning permission for development that is of no greater value than existing use value or indeed less than existing use value. The truth is, however, that applications for planning permission are rarely made with a view to implement a planning permission that is not calculated to enhance value.

Planning permission can be seen to be an enhancement to the 'property' rather than the building and one that creates value. There are further ways of potentially increasing the value of property and before we consider sourcing a site suitable for development it is worth mentioning those as they may offer opportunities to the developer.

4.5 Amendment of leases
Enfranchisement
Leases are not strictly 'real property' having been historically a contract between landlord and tenant but their clear association with real property gives them a classification between chattel and real property, chattels real. Today, few people would make a distinction between leases and real property. We have to remember, however, that a lease gives the right to occupy a building for a set term of years. This right is exclusive, and it is subject to strict terms known as covenants within the lease setting out obligations of both landlord and tenant. Tenant covenants are particularly important as a breach of these terms can in theory lead to forfeiture of the lease.

The Leasehold Reform Act 1967 introduced the opportunity for tenants of houses to enfranchise their leases subject to certain conditions of occupancy and subject to schemes of management implemented by landlords for the benefit of established estates. So, tenants could buy the freehold of the house that they occupied for a value calculated as a capitalisation of the ground rent together with the present value of the reversion. Section 1 of the Leasehold Reform and Urban Development Act 1993 introduced collective enfranchisement that gave the right for tenants of flats to collaborate and purchase the freehold of their residential block of flats subject to a majority of them wishing to do so.

Enfranchisement can therefore be a financial benefit to a leaseholder as a successful acquisition of the freehold interest in a property will generally enhance value, potentially by a greater amount than the cost of the acquisition. This is 'property development' of a kind but it does not involve construction.

Extinguishment of tenants' covenants
Tenants' covenants imposed with the object of making a development more desirable may become obsolete over time.

In 1975 it may have seemed that flats in a new block would be more desirable if all were subject to a restriction on sub-letting, thereby conferring an exclusivity where they were occupied by the tenants of the flats themselves paying a ground rent and service charges to a shared management company. As time has passed, however, and more people work abroad, legislation with the Housing Act 1988 makes the letting of flats easier and rental values increase, so the tenants of these flats start to question whether they wish to continue with this restriction. Inevitably there are some that do and some that do not but eventually the restriction is removed and all flat owners are freed of the restriction on sub-letting. This change enhances value and one has to acknowledge that enhancement is due to the changes in society. Change such as vocational mobility, legislation and increased rental values have trumped the original desire to create an exclusive block of flats occupied by leaseholders.

There may indeed be other covenants within the leases of flats in a block, the freehold of which is owned by a management company owned by the leaseholders, the amendment or extinguishment of which might enhance value to the benefit of all.

The most obvious is ground rent which may be of considerable benefit to an absent freeholder but might have a negative effect on the value of the flats owned by the leaseholders. This is particularly so with 'escalating' ground rents.

Again, these activities could be termed 'property development' but they do not involve construction.

4.6 Site sourcing

'To strive, to seek, to find... and not to yield.'

The quotation comes from Tennyson's Ulysses. The final four words are often missed in quotation and overlooked in practice.

So, the first activity of the developer will be to source a project suitable for development. Let us remind ourselves what this requires. The GDV (Gross Development Value) of the project must be greater than the site or building acquired, together with the costs of undertaking the development, construction, fees and finance and not forgetting a profit. Few people will undertake a development project with all the effort, skill and risk this involves merely to improve the environment. It must be clear. Do the figures genuinely anticipate a return of 15% on GDV or more? If the answer is no, there is no point in going ahead.

The sourcing of development projects requires instinct, time, energy and strategy. The developer will need some instinct as to what makes a potential residential development site, but I suspect that it is precisely this that has drawn the reader to undertake a residential development project and to be reading this book. If they have no instinct for it, they will no doubt have no wish to do it. It will need time allocated to the search. You cannot merely turn up at an estate agent and be handed a list of development projects available to purchase. Sourcing sites takes a great deal of time. Housebuilders employ full time professionals to do this who are often qualified chartered surveyors or town planners with huge experience in site sourcing. If a developer is not prepared to spend some time on this activity what chance do they have in competition with these professionals?

The would-be developer will need to be energetic. As one housebuilder put it to me, 'This business is often about being in the right place at the right time. It helps to be in all the places all of the time'. The developer must make contacts, aware that they are in the market to acquire projects all the time. If a developer is recognised as a 'player' they will have agents contacting them.

Strategy is vital – planning and directing the acquisition, project management and construction of a residential development project in a methodical and measured way and a strategy for sales of the completed houses that ensures success and profitability.

To source projects you first need to decide where to concentrate your efforts. It serves no purpose spreading the net widely. It generally makes more sense for the residential developer to select a geographical area that they are to operate in. Clearly it is best to select somewhere that they are familiar with. The local area where they are known will no doubt be best. Working in a local area may allow the developer to hear of opportunities from acquaintances and friends. Working locally will help build up knowledge of an area and perhaps the developer will become someone who local people contact when they are considering selling property.

A useful boundary for a geographical area is a local authority boundary. Let's say you decide to focus on just three London boroughs or district councils. This will enable you to understand the planning policies in certain boroughs or district council areas and even get to understand the preferences of certain councillors on the planning committees if you take the trouble to attend them. Local developers may even be invited by the planning authority to attend planning forums that create policy. Not all planners work in ivory towers and many welcome the views of local developers. Attempting to buy sites in unknown areas where values are not understood, where you are not in touch with local demand and have no knowledge of local planning policy can be a recipe for disaster. It is important to build up contacts in a selected area and network as much as possible.

Estate agents, lawyers and architects will be the developer's first contacts. The developer will find that the more they are visible in an area the more estate agents and others will come to them with development opportunities. A board on a site stating that 'further sites are required in this area' is the very best, and cheapest, way of getting further sites. Of course, a glamorous website is a must. It does not require too much detail but photographs of past and current projects will create credibility and interest. Property network events are a good way of spreading the word. Many attendees may not be developers themselves and may wish to collaborate or recommend introductions.

You should always be aware that the deal is as important as the site. That is to say that it is not good to overpay for the most attractive site in the best area. Better to consider the deal. What is the vendor's motivation? Is there a crucial timescale to be observed? Does the vendor wish to limit the proposal in some way such as a reduction of dwelling numbers or height of buildings? Can accommodation works (improvement of retained property) be offered to the vendor? Does the vendor wish to be involved in the development, for example by taking some of their land value from profits such as a percentage of the sale price? Is an immediate payment such as increased consideration for an option an incentive? An open mind to consider alternatives is important.

4.7   Introducing agents as site finders

I have mixed feelings about introducing agents. If you are introduced to a highly profitable deal then why should you not pay the introducing agent? I have often found, however, that introducing agents have the impression that the mere advising of the availability of a project is enough to warrant a substantial fee. I do not agree. To my mind an introducing agent should be prepared to put together information about the project and to handle the acquisition negotiation on behalf of the developer. They are then worth their fee and I would never resent that. When I say a fee, I mean 2% to 2.5% of the purchase price of the site paid upon completion of the purchase. I do not mean a share of the profit of the project which is to be created by the multiple and complex activities of the development team. There is so much more to a successful project than its acquisition, notwithstanding the importance of the identification and negotiation involved in the acquisition process. However, there are times when, conscious of the sensitivity of a negotiation, the involvement of an intermediary introducing agent can be very beneficial.

4.8   Controlling the acquisition

Whoever is handling the acquisition it is important to be in control of the process and its timing. Control means that the developer sets out the timescale. They may offer the vendor to have his lawyer draft the legal agreement. They set out any requirement that the vendor will need to action, for example seeking a mortgagee's consent to a sale of part may take time and hold up the transaction if not identified at the outset and undertaken expeditiously. Matters such as this should be addressed when terms are agreed and timescales discussed, not left to the week before exchange of the purchase contract.

4.9   Identifying the key issues

When investigating the development potential of a project there will always be one or two 'key issues' that need to be understood or resolved prior to any further investigation and work is incurred on the project. These might relate to just about anything. Commonly, 'Is there the realistic likelihood of achieving the desired planning permission?' or 'What is the extra over cost of the retaining walls likely to be?' Less commonly, 'Can we indemnify the potential enforcement of the restrictive covenant?' or 'What on earth is the neighbour doing with twenty old cars rotting in his back yard?'

Key issues need to be addressed before any others and this means that the due diligence process is not a methodical ticking of boxes. Some issues will demand to be addressed prior to others. The developer needs to have the ability to recognise these key issues and to prioritise them. There is no point in commissioning a land survey and architect's plans for a project that is, for example, subject to a building scheme restrictive covenant which is likely to defeat all potential for development. The developer may not wish to instruct a lawyer until the cost of the retaining walls on a sloping site is quantified or the results of a pre-application meeting with planners is known.

All development projects will have key issues. The developer must be sure to identify them and be prepared to walk away from a deal if there is no solution to them.

4.10   Due diligence

Readers may be familiar with the 'long form', the list of questions that have to be answered for a company acquisition. It is called the long form because it is long and it is the due diligence required for that process. The term 'due diligence' has been borrowed in recent years to describe the investigative process required for project acquisition. A project acquisition is perhaps not quite as daunting as a company acquisition but certainly it is good practice to prepare a pre-contract report that requires a list of questions to be answered such that all matters are documented and reviewed prior to the acquisition taking place. When I worked for a national house builder the review process included a pre-contract meeting where the land buyer sat at the end of a table alongside heads of departments, all experts in their own fields, ready to interrogate the land buyer on every aspect of the project. It was almost inevitable that the project would not suit one of them. The sales director would raise eyebrows on the projected sales prices, the engineer would be concerned about the extra over costs of foundations or drainage, the lawyer might grumble about a risky title. The bottom line was, as they all knew, that every project has its risks. If it does not, that is probably because the land buyer had not recognised it. Risks, then, are identified by the due diligence and a strategy put in place to overcome them.

4.11   Collating information

Maintaining a well ordered filing system is an important part of the acquisition strategy. The land buyer will need to maintain files of sites they are considering and those they have looked at and for some reason had to put to one side. They should not throw away details of sites that have been rejected until it is known that another developer is building them out. It is surprising how often opportunities for projects reappear and if one has information on them it could be useful. The file should retain details of telephone numbers and addresses, sketches, reports and any copies of information that became available while investigating the site. Keeping details of the offer date and terms could also be helpful.

As an example, a telephone number of a relative in Scotland noted on a file once gave me the advantage to pursue a site many had given up on. The site's owner had taken herself off to live in Inverness. The site became a very successful development.

Seeing potential in property takes experience. The dilapidated building on a good sized plot has an obvious potential. Often, however, a great many letters will already have been posted through that door over the years from developers who have also identified that potential.

Economic obsolescence is less obvious. It occurs when a building, for reasons of its design or use, simply does not command a high value notwithstanding its condition. The land value can in such cases be more than the value of the existing building and so might, subject to achieving planning permission, be a development project. Such buildings are less likely to have been identified by developers.

4.12   Site assembly

Site assembly is the process of putting a number of land interests together to make up an area suitable for a development site. This may mean parts of two or three rear gardens to make a site for just one new house or it might mean a complex assembly of legal interests, freehold, leasehold and third party rights such as fresh easements and sight lines, or extinguishment of existing rights, to create a much larger site for a multiple housing scheme. Site assembly tests the acquisition skills of the developer. There is inevitably much negotiation involved and it is interesting to experience the wide range of attitudes and motivations in the intending vendors with whom the negotiations are conducted. There are often unequal timing requirements. An urgency to sell from one vendor is almost inevitably countered by an inability to go ahead immediately by another. Then there is the 'recalcitrant'. Do they really not wish to sell or are they holding out for a higher price? This is a question I cannot answer, only to say that in my experience not everyone 'has their price'.

Site assembly is one of the great skills of the land buyer and it often results in the acquisition of a site at a more favourable price than an open market purchase of a site that has been assembled given the personal involvement of the land buyer in negotiating with each seller separately.

There are a few rules to follow in a site assembly. The first is to secure the tranche of land that is the key to the planned site. This will tend to exclude the competition who will not then wish to acquire the remaining tranches of land. This key tranche can be secured by way of purchase, contract or option and clearly the developer who is prepared to put money down and purchase is in a strong position. The next rule is to be prepared to work with the least number of tranches of land notwithstanding that the opportunity exists to acquire a great many more tranches. If a development can be carried out with just three tranches the developer should not delay by attempting to negotiate further land even though that is the longer term intention. The next rule is to control the negotiation by dealing with each vendor separately where this is possible.

In addition, it should be appreciated that it is often not only freehold land that needs to be assembled to make up the site. There may be easements for laying drainage or sight lines for egress (exit) across neighbouring properties. These are third party rights and they can sometimes be just as important as the land that makes up the substance of the site.

4.13   Planning history

Knowing the planning history of a project can be crucial. It could be that where an intending vendor has failed to secure planning permission on several occasions, they are likely to welcome an approach from a professional developer willing to take a chance at their own expense. This may give the developer an opportunity to acquire the site on favourable terms. I have very recently developed a site where two planning applications had been made that I considered had completely missed the point and were unlikely to have ever been supported by the planners given the very clear guidance in the local plan. My own proposals recited precisely the objectives of the local plan so were approved without amendment. Consider then that I was able to acquire the site upon favourable terms but also, and importantly, I was pretty sure that I was not wasting time and money on a chance planning application.

I highly recommend investigating the planning history prior to agreeing terms. This can be done very simply by viewing the local planning authority website.

4.14   Negotiating

The object of the negotiation is to agree terms and a purchase price for the site. Often this will involve agreeing the terms of the acquisition and a heads of terms document is prepared to pass to the lawyers on both sides recording the agreement. We never take 'no deal' off the table. If the vendor believes that the developer will do the deal in any event, the developer has destroyed any advantage they may have had. Donald Trump has said that, '*The worst thing you can possibly do in a deal is seem desperate to make it. That makes the other guy smell blood, and then you're dead.*'

Negotiating is an art but there is some advice I can give. One must always understand that some vendors will be keen to sell, and some will be keen only if the buyer is prepared to overpay for the site. Most development sites come with drawbacks, possibly even risks. The land buyer's task then is to identify these issues and to persuade the vendor that they are able to overcome them. A simple example is obtaining planning permission. Where a vendor has been offered a sum for a site subject to obtaining a planning permission for a scheme that is in a developer's opinion unrealistic, it is perfectly in order to say so. It may be that this is what the vendor wants to hear as they wish to dispose of the site swiftly and do not wish to hang around waiting for a planning permission that is unlikely to materialise. OK, it is equally likely that this vendor wishes to try their luck in obtaining the consent and the enhanced value. A refusal of planning permission in such circumstances will, however, give an opportunity to return to the negotiation.

4.15   Making an offer

The professional way of making an offer is to carefully consider all the costs and ensure that all the viabilities and sketch plans have been prepared. The offer might even attach a copy of plans to a carefully written letter if the deal is to acquire subject to planning permission just to prove that it is the intention to take the matter seriously. Or there is an alternative. I recall one very successful developer who used to visit me when I was a selling agent on the date offers were due and make his offer verbally. He would then judge the reaction and swiftly increase the offer if he felt it needed to be done. Unless the agent states that offers need to be in writing stating various matters to be confirmed you should try to avoid doing so. Too much information is sometimes what vendors are persuaded by but in my opinion most focus on the offer price. Rarely is the vendor's decision made straightaway. It may need to be compared to alternative offers if there are a number of conditions or, indeed, if there are a number of vendors such as a family of relatives, then it may need to be aired among them prior to acceptance. In such circumstances the vendor or agent may return to the developer seeking confirmation of terms, or commitment to further terms.

The developer should never be too keen to get a deal agreed at any price. Here is where those final four words from Ulysses come in. Often the better deals are 'second time around deals', that is the first offer has failed to go ahead perhaps through inability to obtain finance or planning permission or perhaps because the party of the successful offer now feels they are overpaying for the site. If a developer is contacted by an agent to ask if they will proceed with their offer as the agreed deal has not gone ahead, it is the ideal opportunity to amend the offer slightly, introducing a further requirement such as more time to go ahead or to make the offer subject to an additional condition.

4.16   Offers and acceptance for property

When putting an offer in writing for land it should state that it is subject to contract. This means that it is setting out the terms of the offer but that the terms will not form part of a binding agreement to purchase until they are incorporated in a contract for sale and purchase prepared by lawyers. Contracts for the sale and purchase of land have to be in writing and signed by both parties and they have to incorporate all the agreement in one document. That is to say that any promises made that are not picked up in the contract cannot later be relied upon (see Section 2 Land Registration Act 2002). I will discuss later the requirements of a contract for the purchase of development land which, while incorporating the usual contractual requirements, can usefully incorporate certain contingent conditions that allow for the need for planning permission to be granted.

4.17   Meetings

If a developer is called to discuss proposals at a meeting with an intending vendor, perhaps with their advisors, it is as well for them to go properly prepared. It is said that there is no point in having a meeting without an agenda. I agree, and I would go one step further. It is beneficial for the developer to prepare that agenda. In that way they may steer the meeting to acknowledge their points. They should bring any backup material that will support their case such as comparative sales, legal opinions or construction costings. I have always found that if a plan of the proposed development has been prepared, this is an effective centrepiece to the discussion.

It is always good to stick to the agenda and take notes marking who is to action the various points agreed. At the end of the meeting the developer should summarise the action to be undertaken and confirm that they will email the meeting notes to the vendor or their advisor. In this way they will find the deal moving forward rather than being subject to an ambling discussion centred around the intending vendor's principal concern. The meeting notes should be dated and filed.
'

4.18   Buying property at auction

Today all types of property are sold at auction and all types of vendors use auctions to dispose of surplus properties. The benefit of an auction sale to a vendor is the knowledge that the best price available on the day has been achieved and the certainty of the sale having effectively exchanged the contract on the fall of the auctioneer's hammer. The benefit of the auction purchase to the buyer is the potential of a 'steal' if there are no competitive bids in the room and again the certainty of having acquired a project. Buying property at auction thereby has the speculative element some buyers are attracted to. Will there be competition in the room? Will certain lots be knocked down at bargain prices? Given the set timescale of commitment to an auction purchase the buyer should take care to investigate the lots they are interested in.

Viewing the property
The auctioneer will produce a legal pack prepared by the seller's solicitor for inspection by the intending buyers. Arrangements are usually made for viewing days where the building or land can be inspected and it is essential that the buyer views the property before committing themselves to buying it at auction.

Investigation
When carrying out due diligence of property offered at auction the buyer has to bear in mind that the bid for a lot at auction is accepted when the hammer comes down and is a commitment to purchase the lot. The auctioneer's clerk will ask the bidder to sign a contract and to pay a deposit at this point. Due diligence prior to entering the 'room' should therefore be thorough.

Legal pack
A legal pack will be prepared for every property offered at auction. It is important to read and understand the legal pack. This is the 'property' that is being offered for sale and therefore the legal rights and responsibilities are the essence of it. I am often amazed to hear of developers and investors who buy at auction without having paid sufficient attention to the legal pack. I have even known of one party who bought a property with a short term remaining on its lease unaware that he was not buying a freehold. I can only assume that he made the classic error of buying a building rather than a property, oblivious to the rights and responsibilities he inherits as owner.

Is it mortgageable?
A matter the developer may need to give attention to is whether the building they are to bid on is mortgageable. If they are relying on finance it may be that the lender will seek to retain some part of the acquisition funding while certain repairs have taken place. Indeed, it is possible that the property is, for some reason, not of a kind that would offer sufficient security for a mortgage. This would present a problem to a buyer who has exchanged a contract for its purchase.

Buying pre-auction

It is quite common to see certain lots entered into a catalogue and marked as sold prior to the auction taking place. This could be seen as a way of encouraging bidders to alternative lots but it is quite possible that since the catalogue was printed, a successful sale of that lot came about as a buyer wished to prevent the lot being offered to a wider market. It is therefore possible for a developer to arrange a purchase prior to an auction taking place.

Buying post-auction

If a lot fails to reach its reserve price there is the opportunity to approach the auctioneer to buy by way of private treaty. Indeed, if the buyer has shown an interest when 'in the room' the auctioneer may well approach them following a failure to reach the reserve price to discuss a deal. The buyer is in the position of having seen the failure of the sale and can therefore potentially secure the lot for a favourable price.

I have had great success in selling at auction but I confess I have never bought property at auction. I have certainly purchased post-auction sale when a lot failed to reach a reserve price. This can be very advantageous to a buyer as the vendor has incurred auction fees and failed to sell and is therefore likely to be minded to reduce their price to secure a deal.

4.19   Buying property by tender

It has been said that when there is a high level of demand for a property, tender is the best way to achieve the highest price. Tenders may be contractual where all tenderers agree to submit bids on the basis that one will be accepted and a contract exchanged, or they may be non-contractual. I have not seen contractual tenders for many years and I recall that when I did, they were for quality residential sites in sought after areas and in sellers' markets.

Informal tenders

More common today is the informal tender which is where all tenderers submit their best offers but these offers remain subject to contract. This leaves open the due diligence process though intending buyers are often required to confirm that they have thoroughly investigated the project and to prove that they have funds to proceed.

Design tenders

Design tenders are generally used by local authorities or development corporations who are not only interested in the price they are to receive but also the design of the project that the price is based on. The idea is to ensure that a high level of design is not compromised, particularly where further sites and projects are to be sold by the authority to be developed in the general area. The developer will need to work with an architect in formulating such a tender as plans will be submitted to the vendor's advisors along with the price the developer is proposing to pay.

4.20   Instructing lawyers

A transaction for the transfer of property has to comply with rules set out in various statutes that dictate procedure and formality. A contract will be entered into between the parties followed by the transfer of the property from seller to buyer. The contract has to be in writing and it will identify the property, the parties and the intention to create a legally binding agreement for sale and purchase. This will be signed, i.e. 'exchanged' by both parties. This is referred to as exchange of contracts because in practice each party will probably sign a separate contract which are then exchanged between the parties' lawyers.

The transfer is the deed that follows the contract. It will contain the rights and responsibilities (covenants) together with the plan that is to be submitted to the Land Registry.

When a lawyer is to act in the acquisition of property they will need to be aware of the project proposals so that any legal restrictions of any kind that would inhibit their implementation are known about.

What are the intentions? The lawyer will be drafting or approving a contract or option agreement so it is essential that they are advised of the terms of the deal. There may be a proposal to allocate communal facilities within the project that will require properties to be granted rights for their use and an obligation to meet part of the costs of maintenance. There may be proposals to extend the site at a later date with the acquisition of contiguous land. Rights of access and easements for services will need to be reserved.

What is the timescale? Is there a wish to exchange a contract as soon as possible or to delay exchange until other matters are settled? There may be time limits within legal documentation that should be taken into account such as an overage clause. Is the acquisition to be conditional? Is the proposal to access further contiguous land?

Is the intention that estate road and drainage be adopted by the local authorities? If this is to be the case, adoption agreements will have to be drawn up by the local authority lawyer and approved by the lawyer acting for the developer.

What is the identity of the acquisition company? Should this need to be altered prior to completion for any reason it will be advisable, for the avoidance of doubt, to have an alienation clause in the contract which allows you to assign the contract if necessary.

The lawyer needs to know who the funders are and which lawyer will be representing them. The acquisition will require approval from the lawyer acting for the funder and there will be a number of documents that the developer and the funder need to agree.

4.21   Heads of terms
It is useful for the developer to carefully consider a heads of terms in instructing their lawyer setting out all the above in clear and considered terms. Failure to do so may result in omission of some important aspect of the developer's intention.

Case study 1
Acquisition of development site
Key Issue: Planning agreement for allocation of homes for affordable housing.

Facts of the case study
Planning permission had been granted for 33 homes on an old school site in a seaside town in Kent. The development would involve refurbishment of an old ragstone school building and the construction of new housing. A number of the houses were to be affordable.

Analysis of the issues for the acquisition team
The planning authority favoured small residential units with limited car parking.

The existence of buildings on the site created a high existing use value and a high level of SDLT.

VAT is payable on the cost of restoration work though at a reduced rate where the school was being converted to residential use.

A housing association would have to be brought in to the deal as a registered provider would be required to take the affordable housing element of the scheme.

The vendor was the County Council.

The sales market in the small seaside town was judged to be slow.

Decision
These facts pointed the acquisition team to submit the scheme to a small number of housing associations as a package deal for the following reasons.

(1)   The vendor had to acquiesce to a delay in the purchase timing given the affordable housing element in any event. There was thereby no disadvantage in advising the vendor that the housing association would be taking the whole scheme, albeit that there would be a delay.

(2)   A private scheme could take some time to sell particularly with limited car parking and the presence of affordable housing within the development.

(3)   A registered provider would not pay SDLT for such a scheme.

(4)   The developer would not need to provide funding for the scheme as this would be provided upon monthly valuations by the housing association.

These facts pointed to a scheme for affordable housing and the result was a very successful development.

Case Study 2
Site acquisition
Key issue: Sourcing development opportunities.

I have found that the key to sourcing development opportunities is to be the 'player' in a certain area. The developer who is carrying out a project in a specific area is more likely to be approached by the vendor or agent seeking the buyer of another site in that area. The agent will know that the developer who is on site close by will have navigated the planning and related restrictions and requirements and is most likely to be successful in securing a planning permission. This is the principal way in which sites are sourced. So how does the developer start the process? They must identify the potential for their first development and have assembled a site themselves. If they have done so without the assistance of an agent then they are 'agent free' for the sales of the property which will enable them to court local agents keen to be instructed on the sales.

I have, throughout my career, always carried information on a number of development opportunities. These need not be under any kind of option or obligation to sell but collecting information on them should they materialise as an acquisition is important. Potential sites can be released for any number of reasons. There is enforced sale through death or divorce but also a single transaction in the market can inspire a sale.

I recall such a situation where my colleague became aware of a sale in the market that shed new light on the potential of a site that had been put to one side for a period of time. The sale effectively revalued the estimated selling process of the three houses that would result from the development increasing the land value to a level attractive to the landowner and enabling the acquisition to take place.

The lesson here is to keep in touch with the market. What is being sold? How much is being achieved?

Chapter 5

Designing the residential development project

'Design is not just what it looks like and feels like. Design is how it works.'

This great quotation is from a great man, Steve Jobs.

Let's look at how design is so important in residential development projects. Design of new buildings or the renovation of existing buildings is of course an integral part of operational development. It plays a vital part in the assessment of the value of the new homes to be built in terms of the density of the development, the accommodation provided and the appearance of the buildings. The design has to be aesthetically pleasing but also it has to work. A building, after all, has to provide shelter, heating, lighting and power, privacy, security and comfort. It is often the case that simple and repetitive design with the use of what the architect Eric Lyons used to call 'common denominators' is the best solution in new housing projects, especially when combined with high quality materials and landscaping. The developer may often prefer to implement simple design to save cost and time of construction work.

Design can create densities of development that optimise land use in cities where demand is high, often by limiting car parking and increasing the height of new buildings. Design can solve problems in a layout and save costs by limiting expensive and unnecessary construction works such as retaining walls and access roads. Design can add value to a scheme boosting the GDV and profit. Good design can be what wins over the planners and local people to achieve the grant of planning permission.

The architect is the lead consultant. They will coordinate information with other consultants and monitor the satisfaction of planning conditions and building regulations.

A good architect not only designs the project but guides the developer through the planning process, condition requirements and building regulations. They will have worked and be working on similar schemes and be conversant with planning requirements and the latest trends. They will deal with other professionals as their contacts and be able to recommend professionals for the flood risk assessment or the ecology report that planners have demanded.

So, the advice has to be to use a good architect who has experience in the area the developer is working in.

5.1　　Sketch schemes

I have always found a basic sketch scheme to be a useful prerequisite to making an offer to buy a site. This is often something the developer can prepare themselves. A few sheets of tracing paper and pencil will be enough to sketch up an idea of the proposals sufficient to establish a value and proposal. If one is artistic enough to glamourise it a little, then the tabling of an attractive layout plan will have a positive impact in any meeting with the vendor or planner. I have always drawn basic schemes to a 1:500 scale using standard house designs.

Standard house designs

Many developers have a catalogue of standard house types. This does not need to be extensive and indeed should not be. A small number of designs put together by an experienced architect following the developer's instructions will help focus efforts when sourcing plots. I recall my colleague having a design drawn up after recognising that in an area close to us, plots were all a certain width. A replacement dwelling would have to fit on that plot width and thus the design was of a five bedroom house with integral garage and a family room extension to the rear. It became one of our most popular house types which was repeated time and again. Repeating designs helps avoid errors and costs, so it is good to use standard house types where possible. Repetition will help a developer to see what works and what does not. Specification will also be repeated, making pricing easier. The design team will study the finished house to see where improvements and cost savings can be made which are sometimes difficult to see on plan.

It may even be possible to get an idea of selling price if the same design has been recently sold locally. So, a portfolio of standard house types is recommended.

Standard house designs are useful in drawing up sketch layout plans. The standard design footprints should be drawn to a scale of 1:500 on a separate piece of tracing paper so that one can simply pencil over the outline onto a proposed layout plan. This will save time and avoid inaccuracy. The layout will need to consider design criteria such as height, massing, minimum separation and garden lengths and of course there will be limitations of the site itself. The layout plan will therefore only be indicative at this stage, ignoring limitations like trees and ground levels. A basic sketch will, however, help to focus attention on the viability of the proposals as well as the potential limitations.

Working up the sketch layout

The sketch layout plan will form the basis of the instruction to the architect so that they may prepare the planning drawings following receipt of the site survey plan. It may be that the initial sketch scheme is judged to be a little ambitious at this stage, but it will in my view be worth time preparing something that represents the initial thoughts prior to instructing an architect as it may mean that money on abortive fees is not wasted if the deal does not go ahead.

In choosing an architect, it must be borne in mind that the developer will, following grant of planning permission, be instructing the architect to draw up working drawings for building regulation approval and on site construction purposes. It is as well to be sure that the architect can do this and remember that most site based personnel like clear construction plans that contain enough but not too much information. The project team should scrutinise plans for positioning of electrical points, boiler, radiator positions and waste pipes particularly in the kitchen.

If there is uncertainty about the locating or sizing of services then instructing a mechanical engineer will solve the problem. They will need working drawings to mark up with the services and connections. Failure to undertake a thorough examination of the plans can result in trying to fit a washing machine against a wall only to find there is no waste connection.

5.2 Specifications

The specification is part of the design. The technical input is provided by the architect and should be of a standard that can be used to obtain quotations from subcontractors and suppliers. The specification will be read with the drawings and an obvious point is to ensure that each seeks the same result.

It is useful to prepare specifications of the materials and finishes of the project so that the project manager can begin to think through the programme period and the costs. Specifications that include photographs of fittings together with the descriptions and sources are particularly useful. It is usual to prepare a specification in two stages; an initial specification will help prepare costs and budgets and will also help with the sales survey, and then a final specification that is a useful document in obtaining quotations from subcontractors and in preparing details for the sale of the property.

5.3   Kitchen layouts

It will be useful to have a kitchen layout agreed at an early stage in the construction process. This will help with the location of service connections prior to first fix to avoid absence of drainage outgoes, water supply and electrical points. It will also mean that the cost of kitchens is agreed early in the process and an attractive drawing will be prepared by the kitchen designer to lodge with the estate agent enhancing the potential of achieving off plan sales.

5.4   Bathroom plans

I always use a bathroom design company to supply and fit the sanitary ware. Attempts to cut costs with supply-only sanitary ware suppliers have always ended unfavourably. Today I apply the same rule as with the kitchen. Have an experienced designer handle designing, sourcing and fitting the whole bathroom. Additional items to consider might be extractor fans, heated mirrors and towel rails.

5.5   Engineers' design

There are consultant engineers who will supply drawings, calculations and specifications for structural work and civil work. Also, there are a number of engineers' designs that will be supplied as part of a package of design manufacture, supply and fit, for example renewable energy installations and piling design. It is usual for the developer to obtain from these engineers some form of product and design guarantee or a collateral warranty to cover the design if it fails at a later stage.

5.6   Drainage and roads

A civil engineer is a consultant. They will design the foul and surface water drainage system. In many cases this will be a simple drain connecting to an existing manhole on site that leads to an established adopted sewer outside the frontage to the site. In many cases drainage can be a great deal more complicated with submersible pumps for foul drains connected to rising mains to a discharge manhole, surface water storage systems on site moderating surface water discharge. Designs for these should be covered by a collateral warranty.

5.7   Structural design and calculations

The structural engineer is the consultant who will ensure that the development is structurally sound. They will review the architect's design to check loadings, specify foundations and structural components such as blocks for interior walls. They will specify steels to take loadings over wide spans and reinforcement in floor slabs where there may be potential for heave of subsoils.

5.8 Mechanical and electrical design

It is quite possible where a small residential development project is being designed to avoid instructing a mechanical and electrical (M&E) engineer. The architect will show positions of radiators, tanks and electrical plugs and points on working drawings, and a professional subcontractor will be capable of designing layouts to comply with these drawings. Heating systems are often designed by a specialist working for the plumbing contractor so the requirement for an M&E contractor is less. However, the developer may wish to instruct a professional to handle the connection of services, internal layouts and the issue of SAP (Standard Assessment Procedure) ratings and EPCs (Energy Performance Certificates) for practical completion.

5.9 Piling and floor slab design

In my experience short bored piling is becoming more common for residential development sites. This is where piles are set into a borehole rather than driven into the ground. This may be due to cost. Piling creates less excavated soil than a deep dig strip foundation and the cost of 'muck away', the removal of soil, has risen more than many building costs over the last few years. The cost of piling, therefore, looks more competitive than it used to. It may be due to innovative design. Today, professional piling contractors provide piles and cast in situ floor slabs as one operation avoiding the need for ground beams and block floors. This allows the contractor to rely on just one subcontractor and supplier for the operation. Increased use of industrial sites has no doubt brought about the use of suspended cast in situ slabs where any ground gases are rendered harmless by a void under the slab itself. So too can ground water effects be mitigated by a raised ground floor slab. Foundations in close proximity to existing buildings can cause difficulties. One way of accommodating this is to construct a cantilevered reinforced concrete slab on piles driven away from the existing wall. So, there are a number of reasons why this method of piling has become more common. A more cynical view is that perhaps the increased use of piling is simply a desire to reduce risk of foundation failure.

5.10 Timber frame design

Timber frame manufacturers are specialists in the design of structures that can incorporate high levels of acoustic, fire and thermal insulation. The timber frame forms the structural component of the building and external walls can be clad with conventional brick or blockwork, timber boarding or tiling. An advantage of timber frame is the speed of construction especially when the supplier undertakes the construction work themselves. Off site design has the advantage of avoiding waste and most timber frames include external insulations within the panels avoiding any surplus supply.

5.11   Roof truss design

Working drawings will need to be submitted to a roof trusses company for design and fabrication of roof trusses and a price quotation. This should be done at least four weeks in advance of intended delivery. It is possible to have the carpenter cut and pitch the roof structure but I like to rely on a truss manufacturer for this as design will be under their guarantee.

The roof structure of the dwelling should be inspected by the building inspector prior to felt and battening taking place.

5.12   Solid floor design

Solid concrete floors at first floor level give a house a special feel. Sound transmission is significantly reduced and I will always fit a solid floor in a luxury masonry built detached house. A solid floor can be formed of hollow planks or beam and blocks. My preference is for the hollow planks which can be craned into position on delivery by the supplier avoiding the need for additional labour to place blocks.

5.13   Renewable energy design

Renewable energy is that created on site rather than that taken off the grid. It has many forms. The most common used for residential schemes is photovoltaic (PV) panels. These are invariably fitted to the roof of a house and contribute to, rather than provide the energy for, the building. Photovoltaic panels are relatively cheap to install and are in some districts required as part of the planning permission. I try to resist fitting PV panels to the front roof of the house as I consider this to be unsightly.

It is worth considering fitting the panel frames to the roof structure prior to felt and battening rather than on the completed roof.

5.14   Specification

If the developer is lucky enough to secure a buyer off plan they will no doubt need to attach a specification of the unfinished house to the contract. The developer must be cautious when including specifications in legal documentation. If an item is overlooked in construction they will wish to avoid a buyer pointing out that it was included in a specification attached to their contract.

5.15   Practicality of design

The developer has to consider the practicality of design. It may look beautiful but will it sell? It is often said that the developer has to remember that they are not building a house for their own occupation but one that is to be sold on the market. Personal touches are not always appreciated and standard features are often the better approach. I recall building an estate of houses on a sloping site with split level floors. Everyone who viewed liked the appearance of those houses and commented favourably on the split levels, but they took some time to sell. The problem was that, while buyers liked the split level when viewing, in considering the effect when living in those houses they did not consider them practical.

Case study 3

Key issue: Appropriate design close to a listed building or conservation area.

In my experience, design of buildings is rarely a key issue that makes or breaks a planning proposal. I have seen many outstanding and sympathetic designs refused planning permission and rather ordinary and unimaginative designs given approval. It is always a pleasure, however, to see a case where intelligent design overcomes an objection. In the case of listed buildings and conservation areas the design of housing within their vicinity can be a sensitive issue. There is a school of thought that historic buildings are better complemented by modern design that does not attempt in any way to mimic the historic building. Others may argue that the developer should incorporate some feature in recognition of the listed building or conservation area. In one case I was faced with a project between a conservation area and a rather ordinary housing estate originally built as council housing. What design was appropriate? The plain and rather cheaper built sixties council housing or the conservation area houses? I elected to build housing that reflected the conservation area in terms of materials used such as clay hanging tiles and stock brick. In this way the project was literally between the two, an upgrade from the sixties housing but without the intricacy of the houses in the conservation area.

Chapter 6

Valuing the site for the project

'It's not hard to make decisions when you know what your values are.'
Roy Disney

I am certain that Roy Disney did not give us this quotation with residential development project values in mind but I am borrowing it anyway as, while taken out of context, it seems to me to fit. We have to have a feel of the numbers at an early stage in order to make our decisions as to how, and indeed whether, to proceed.

In order to get a feel of the potential of the site and how much it is likely to cost to buy, a developer carries out a simple residual valuation. The idea is to deduct all costs including normal profit from the gross development value (the total sales income) to establish the residue. This sets out the approximate figures such that it can be seen whether the deal 'stacks up'.

A simplified residual valuation will show:	%	%
Projected Gross Development Value	100	
Less: Costs of sale		2
Build cost		40
Fees		7
Finance (fees and interest)		12
Profit		15
Residual land value		24
Total	100	100

It will be seen from this elementary calculation that the residual land value is what is left after all costs are deducted from the gross development value. It will be seen, too, that I have deliberately used a GDV of 100. From this will be seen typical percentages applying to the figures in the residual valuation, resulting here in a residual land value of 24%.

These percentages will not be appropriate to every calculation. The land cost will tend to be a higher percentage in high class areas, with the build cost percentage being lower, as build costs do not change much from one area to another while sale prices do.

Other factors may come in to play. A sloping site will incur a higher build cost. A risky venture may require a higher profit than the 15% of GDV shown in this example. If interest rates are high, then finance costs will increase.

If the developer is fortunate enough to be utilising their own funds, they will in the above example receive the 12% finance and the 15% profit and thereby may be happy to increase their bid for the land.

The above percentages are typical, and one may be sure that a residual land valuation in excess of 50% is quite exceptional and is likely to result only if some other input is understated.

A lending bank is unlikely to be impressed with a calculation of this simplicity and the developer should be prepared for more arduous calculations which are referred to later at Paragraph 6.2. This simple residual will, however, likely be the type of calculation that will be in a land buyer's head as they first look over the site and ask themselves the questions: What can I get on here? What will it sell for? How much will it cost to build? Are there abnormal costs? How much can I afford to pay for the site? Is there enough profit to make it worthwhile?

6.1   Sales surveys

A sales survey is undertaken to establish the gross development value that is expected to be achieved from a project. This is usually a visit to five local estate agents taking sketch plans of proposals, house plans and specifications with a view to establishing the sales prices likely to be achieved. This is also a useful exercise to establish which local agent is best equipped to sell the scheme. What resources do they have? Do they seem keen? Do they operate at the right end of the market? Are their valuations in line with others or do they seem to have 'overvalued'?

The sales survey should give a better idea of sales values but one should not be put off if all the agents fail to meet expectations. Agents are most likely correct but that does not mean that the site is in some way undevelopable. It may mean returning to the vendor or their agent with the findings to renegotiate the price. It may mean finding some way of increasing the density of development or altering some other aspect of it to make the numbers work but it is as well to know this from the outset rather than find out just as the completed houses are placed on the market for sale.

The sales survey should be retained on a spreadsheet to be updated as the project progresses. Hopefully a second sales survey as the project is completed when the developer appoints an agent to sell the houses will reveal that the market has risen a little. The developer should be aware, however, that occasionally, and I am pleased to say very occasionally, prices will have fallen over the development period.

6.2   Cashflow viabilities
If the residual valuation is the first stab at calculating how much should be paid for the site, the cashflow viability is the spreadsheet with all the numbers on it. In the ideal world this will include a breakdown of the entire build costs, fees, interest and additional costs. In practice it will not include this breakdown as the costs are as yet unknown so estimates of build cost on a square metre basis are used instead.

The essential inputs remain the same; the GDV (sales prices) less the costs and normal profit with a residual figure shown for the land. It is just that these costs are broken down on the spreadsheet and a cashflow is applied that has accrued a more accurate figure for interest on the project. Note that it is usual for a cashflow viability to apply interest to borrowed funds and invested funds as there is, of course, an opportunity cost to the developer's investment in the project.

6.3   Valuation methods
There are classic valuation methods adopted by chartered surveyors and valuers. In practice a valuation will incorporate more than one of these methods. The surveyor's valuation will certainly refer to comparables but might also include reference to income potential from letting. A professional valuation of a residential development project will certainly include an analysis of construction costs.

Comparable method
This is the method by which the development proposals or indeed any properties to be offered for sale, are valued against comparable properties on the market or recently sold in the area. A comparison of similar properties to those proposed in the project will give an approximate idea of values very rapidly.

Investment method

This is the method of capitalising an income derived from a property at a given yield. In theory then it may not matter what the property is if the income is secure.

The income is capitalised to create a capital value by first calculating the capitalisation rate. The capitalisation rate is 100 divided by the yield percentage.

For example, if the yield percentage is 8%, the capitalisation rate is 100 divided by 8, producing a capitalisation rate of 12.5.

The capitalisation rate should then be multiplied by the annual rental to produce a valuation of the property. So, if the annual rental is £100,000, the capitalised value will be £100,000 multiplied by 12.5 to give a value of £1,250,000.

This capitalisation rate is often referred to as the Years Purchase (YP).

Construction method

A public building such as a civic hall might be valued simply on the basis of construction cost.

Profits method

The profit method of valuation is used for business property where an income is derived from the property, for example a guest house. No doubt a comparable property can be found to have sold nearby but the subject property used as a guest house may be a different value.

Residual method

The residual method of valuation is used to value residential development projects. It should be noted that input from the comparable method will almost inevitably be made in a residual valuation. This is the valuation method that needs to be understood by the developer.

Automated Valuation Models (AVMs)

An automated valuation results from the input of data into a computer. This data will be previous surveyor valuations, comparable data, indexation and perhaps economic data such as indexes of house prices. AVMs are used by mortgage lenders for certain types of residential property usually where the LTV is at a low rate.

6.4   Valuation using hedonic pricing models

This technique separates a property's component characteristics and by regression analysis (the relationship of the variables) determines a value to each and the correlation of each characteristic to the transaction price. This can be used for property that does not produce income where the sum of characteristics is measured or where there are no comparables. It is also useful when equating the cost of a characteristic to that proportion of the transaction price attributable to that characteristic. In its simplest form is it worth spending £20,000 on a swimming pool when the house will sell for an additional £25,000? What is the additional value of a house located in a specific school catchment area? My own view is that such valuation techniques should be regarded with some scepticism.

6.5   Valuations for lending banks

The developer requiring development finance should be aware that the value of the site will need to be verified by the lending bank's surveyor acting as a RICS registered valuer. This is a secured lending valuation not a valuation for marketing purposes as offered without commitment by an estate agent. Valuers are chartered surveyors valuing to rules set out in the Royal Institution of Chartered Surveyors red book of valuation standards. These rules are strict and require the valuer to commit to their valuation such that they will be responsible should it subsequently be revealed to be ambitious. In short, the developer's optimism as to sale prices or building costs may not be endorsed by the bank valuation.

An understanding of how valuations are ascribed is important to the developer. A secured lending valuation will ascribe a value to the GDV from comparable sales made in the local market as reported by local agents and surveyors or today from specialist research companies. The valuer will assess the estimated building costs to see that sufficient amount has been allowed by the developer. They will provide a valuation figure for the land. The loan can then be provided with a facility of 60-65% of GDV with 100% of building costs to be advanced throughout the building programme and any balance amount contributed to the land acquisition upon legal completion of the purchase. The developer's own optimism may not be endorsed by others, either as valuers acting for a lending bank or as sales agents listing houses for sale. I do not mean to imply that the developer is in error but it may be difficult for them to obtain sufficient funds from the lending bank where a 'down valuation' has occurred. The developer has then got to know the values and be realistic as to their expectations of sales prices.

6.6   Overages
An overage is a further payment to a vendor of land made by the buyer in the event of development or further development taking place following completion of the sale and within a defined timescale. Often this will be where a vendor sells a site with planning permission for a certain number of houses but subject to a clause in the sale contract that the developer will pay a further sum if they implement a planning consent for more houses. The overage is registered as a charge on the title and as such runs with the land as an obligation for a set period of years as agreed in the contract. Overage clauses are common to sales of sites by local authorities and statutory authorities.

6.7   Valuation of access
Access to a development is a vital part of a site. What sometimes occurs is the access is a small area of land leading to a much larger area forming the site. The question that then arises is what is the value of the access? The answer has been provided in the Lands Tribunal case of *Stokes v Cambridge Corporation* (1961) 13 P. & C.R. 77 where the value ascribed was one third of the value of the site less its value without the development consent. This is the method recognised by chartered surveyors when valuing access strips and one can see why these are sometimes called ransom strips.

Case study 4
Secured lending valuation
Key Issue: GDV (Gross Development Value).

Specialist lending banks base their funding facilities on GDV. A bank will typically provide loans of up to 65% of GDV. It is often important for the developer to ensure that the GDV is at a level that allows the bank to provide maximum finance possible and this can be an issue if the valuation is not as high as the developer's expectation. A down valuation of a project's GDV by £250,000 could result in a reduction of £162,500 lending.

The bank will appoint a surveyor to value the site and to ascribe a GDV to the project. Surveyors undertaking secured lending valuations will analyse comparable sales in order to ascribe a GDV to the project. The secured lending valuation will also give a commentary on the proposed building costs so the Contract Sum Analysis (a breakdown of costs on a trade basis) provided by the developer or budget build cost should be robust.

Facts of the case study
Here the valuer was a chartered surveyor with a large reputable firm. He had been instructed by the lending bank to value a site for new houses. The issue was that he could not establish any comparable property to support his valuation and thereby his GDV was substantially lower than that anticipated by the developer. This is not an uncommon outcome of bank valuations and one which can have a negative effect on the acquisition of a development site.

Outcome
It was noted that a site of new houses was being constructed nearby and that a revaluation of the subject site should take place when evidence of sales on the nearby site was available. Fortunately, that evidence supported the developer's view that the GDV for the project was projected at a higher level and a revaluation could take place.

Chapter 7

Land use planning

'A clear vision, backed by definite plans, gives you a tremendous feeling of confidence and personal power.'
Brian Tracy

Land use planning is the term given to the allocation of uses of land and buildings. It is significant as development, whether operational or change of use, generally requires planning permission to be granted by the local planning authority. Development permitted under the GPDO is usually of a minor nature although more recently the scope of permitted development has widened to include changes of use of business premises and agricultural buildings to residential use.

The Town and Country Planning Act 1990 states, at section 55(1), 'Development means the carrying out of building, engineering, mining or other operations in, on, over or under land, or the making of any material change in the use of any buildings or other land.'

So, development will usually require approval by the local planning authority and permission issued by it in writing.

7.1 Local planning authorities

Land use planning is governed at first instance by the local planning authority (LPA), part of the local authority for the area. When someone is intending to develop a project they will no doubt need planning permission unless planning is permitted for the proposal or already granted for it. An application will need to be made to the LPA and a decision will be made either to grant planning permission or refuse to grant it by the planning officer or by a planning committee advised by the planning officer. There is the right to appeal against a refusal of the grant of planning permission to the planning inspectorate so all is not lost if the LPA are unprepared to grant consent. Let us look at the process of an application for planning permission for a residential development project.

Online information

In recent years LPAs have become very efficient at uploading information on development applications online. Most LPAs today list information on applications they are currently considering and have online copies of all plans, reports and correspondence. This helps in making information available to interested parties and the public. It is in any event a useful way of getting an understanding of the information, reports, plans and surveys that are required to make a planning application. Indeed, it can be quite daunting to see the amount of effort and cost that goes into making a planning application and one can only conclude that it is as well to have proposals that are likely to meet the approval of the planning officer to save wasting a great deal of time and money. Browsing the LPA website for planning applications is then a useful method of research as to what is required of a planning application and what proposals are likely to be successful.

7.2   Development plans

Local planning authorities will have prepared, and in many cases, had approved by the Inspectorate, a statutory plan setting out the objectives of the authority in achieving a variety of local needs and housing will be one of these needs. Such plans are adopted policy and the Planning and Compulsory Purchase Act 2004 has reinforced the requirement that decisions as to planning applications need to be in accordance with an adopted plan.

It is certainly worth spending some time familiarising yourself with the local plan to get an insight as to policies which will be set out in it. Proposals for development will have to be in accordance with the development plan 'unless material considerations indicate otherwise'. Local plans often comprise more than one document. It is common to see 'guidance notes' and of course you have to consider national policy.

7.3   Local guidance

You should always be aware of local guidance and policies issued by the planning authority. Compliance with such guidance and policies may well make it easier to obtain planning permission, for example, relating to a locally listed building. This may not have the same level of protection as a statutory listed building but local people will consider it important. A village plan written by local residents may be a valuable starting point in establishing what approach should be made to the design and density of development. Many local authorities issue guidance as to neighbourly conduct in construction works such as delivery hours and working arrangements. It is as well to demonstrate that this is understood when submitting an application for planning permission.

7.4   Site history

Establishing what previous applications have been made for development of the site is very useful. The refusal of an application should give an idea what proposals might not be acceptable. For example, if a previous application has been refused for over development then clearly a fresh application for a similar density will be unlikely to be approved. The density should be reduced. If the previous application was rejected as it proposed the felling of trees it should be the objective to design a scheme that seeks to retain the trees.

I once attended a planning meeting to see an application refused for sheltered housing. Clearly the committee did not like the idea of sheltered housing but felt housing to be appropriate. The architect acting for the charity who owned the land did not attend the planning meeting so was presumably unaware of the position as he sought to have an amended sheltered housing scheme approved. When this was also refused, I contacted the charity with an alternative proposal for housing which was successful. Monitoring the applications and looking into the history of the site can be decisive.

7.5   Pre-application advice

The way to obtain an early insight into the likely response of the planning officer to an application for planning permission is to set up a pre-application meeting. Many LPAs offer pre-application advice as to whether proposals for the development of a site are likely to accord with the development plan and be approved by the local planning authority. There is a charge for this service, but I consider it well worth engaging with the planning officer at this stage. It may well save considerable time and expense in the longer term.

The pre-application meeting will often result in a letter of confirmation setting out the policies applicable to the proposal together with comments from statutory consultees such as highways, that will save time when the application is made.

If the result of a pre-application meeting forces the developer to discuss negative comments with the site owner this may allow a modification of expectations for the site which can be beneficial to both parties.

Estoppel by representation is a legal term that prevents a party from contradicting a previous misrepresentation by subsequently attempting to take a fresh opposing position at a later date. It prevents a party from stating a fact or a situation is untrue when they previously represented that they were true. It potentially describes the advice from a planning officer that a proposal is acceptable only for the proposal to become unacceptable at a later date. The question that will be asked is whether the developer was entitled to rely on advice from a planning officer if they acted on it, say by buying the site. It might come as no surprise that pre-application advice is generally worded carefully to exclude the potential for reliance on it by the developer.

7.6   Planning applications

An application for planning permission for development proposals has to be made to the local planning authority and the content of that planning application has to comply with section 62 of the Town and Country Planning Act 1990. These are to:

(a)   be made in a form provided by the LPA;

(b)   include particulars specified in the form and be accompanied by a plan which identifies the land to which it relates and any other plans and drawings and information necessary to describe the development which is the subject of the application; and

(c)   except where the authority indicate that a lesser number is required, be accompanied by three copies of the form and the plans and drawings submitted with it.

When I started in the business, planning applications could comprise a completed form with an ordnance sheet attached to it with the application site outlined in red. I used to present a drawing of the proposal and a covering letter. There was no fee to be paid to the LPA. That was a very full application.

Today things are very different and a typical planning application for residential development contains a great deal more than the statutory requirements of section 62. Studying an application on the LPA website reveals that a great number of plans, surveys and reports are required to be submitted. These surveys and reports will differ according to each application but let us look at what is typically required.

The application may be outline or detailed and the requirements for each will differ.

Outline planning applications
Where permission is sought for the erection of a building the applicant can apply for an outline planning permission. Their application will seek what is a decision in principle subject to further submissions of 'reserved matters'. These reserved matters are defined to be siting, design, external appearance,

means of access and landscaping. Most outline applications will submit details of these reserved matters 'for illustration only'.

Applications for reserved matters have to be submitted within three years of the outline approval or the permission will run out. Today section 62 of the Planning and Compulsory Purchase Act 2004 requires key design principles such as layout, density, height of buildings, access and landscape to be submitted with an outline application. I believe this makes sense. I have always wished to illustrate proposals with drawings and plans to give an idea of the site's potential and I have always believed that the planning committee appreciates this approach.

Detailed planning applications

The LPA will wish to see a great deal of information in support of a detailed planning application. It should be understood that compiling this information can take a considerable amount of time and allowance has to be made for this.

Plans and drawings

The application must be accompanied by drawings making clear the development proposals. For a development of houses these will be a site layout plan showing levels and existing trees and buildings to be demolished together with house floor plans and elevation drawings. Occasionally a drawing of the proposed street scene will be required where perhaps levels of new and existing buildings have to be illustrated. A location plan marked with a North point is a helpful addition.

Topographical survey

The developer will need to have had a topographical survey undertaken in order to have a planning layout prepared. This can be included within the application in order to give perspective to levels and existing features on the site. It will be useful in determining decisions in any construction management plan and just occasionally, it may identify something overlooked by the land buyer.

Tree report

A tree survey is now something LPAs generally require as part of an application for planning permission particularly where tree preservation orders (TPOs) apply to a site. This is a plan showing the location of the trees probably based on the topographical survey plan, and a report as to the condition of the trees and how the proposals can be accommodated without affecting them. The survey will no doubt need to be undertaken by a qualified arboriculturist and submitted with the application in order that the application is even registered by the LPA. Trees subject to tree preservation orders should be noted early on in the site investigation by enquiry of the LPA. TPO trees will generally be protected and may reduce the development potential of the site. If located at the entrance to a site, for example, they may prevent development altogether as they may inhibit access, restrict sight lines or perhaps root damage will be envisaged with the construction of an access road which will cause resistance in granting planning permission. It is important to understand whether trees are protected and how the proposals will preserve trees on a site. We must always bear in mind that trees can provide an attractive feature to a development and should not be regarded as a negative feature.

Ecology survey and report
Statutory protection is afforded to many species under the Wildlife and Countryside Act 1981. Development will require an ecology report to identify the existence of species such as bats, badgers, dormice and newts. Reports will need to be prepared showing measures to mitigate the effect of development on these species. It will also be necessary to obtain licenses from Natural England to undertake work on a site where such species are found. The licence should be applied for by the developer, supported by a report from a specialist ecologist as to the mitigation measures proposed. It should be noted that licences for work close to badger sets may only be issued for work to be undertaken during certain months of the year and bat licences will only allow work in certain months.

Flood Risk Assessments
If a site is located on a flood plain or near a river a flood risk assessment (FRA) will be required. This will usually be undertaken as part of an application for planning permission and is a complex undertaking by a qualified hydrologist. The FRA has to envisage the impact of that once in a blue moon flood and the design should take in the potential of that impact. It is common to see sites close to rivers designed with garaging at ground level and living accommodation above such that the living accommodation is not affected by floods. The Environment Agency (EA) is today the statutory authority responsible for approving development in flood zones and close to rivers. We should not underestimate their authority.

I once had a delightful site close to a river enthusiastically supported by the LPA. It was outside the flood zone but the road leading to it was not. The LPA followed the recommendation of the EA to refuse to grant planning permission notwithstanding their own desire to grant it.

Soils and environmental considerations
Some sites might need to have an environmental survey undertaken prior to submission of the planning application. Typically these will be industrial sites where contamination may have taken place and activities have disturbed subsoils such that the bearing capacity may have been compromised. This survey will involve bore holes to collect soil samples for analysis and make recommendations in respect of soil quality. The soil survey will also analyse the subsoil suitability for foundations. In certain clay soils, for example, piled foundations may be recommended to avoid soil heave (a movement of clay soils due to weather conditions), an issue we are told may increase with climate change.

Highways
The highways department will be a consultee to the planning application. With a great many small applications there will be no highway issues notwithstanding the common complaints of neighbours as to increased highway use. The highway authority will, however, be concerned to see what impact the development will have on the highways, particularly at the egress of the site. Generally, the highway matters that should be attended to are parking within the site, turning of refuse vehicles within the site and sight lines at the egress of the site.

Parking
The architect will be aware that adequate space should be made available for car parking and that the requisite number of spaces are allocated. LPAs will have standards for car parking both in terms of the number of spaces for each house and the dimensions of the car parking spaces. It is usual today to see a requirement for charging of electric vehicles.

Turning areas
Estate roads will need to be designed to allow for vehicles to turn inside the site. It is usual to show a radius on the site plan that accords with the local highways requirement illustrating the ability for vehicles to turn within the site.

Some local authorities have some very large refuse vehicles, and they will often not be prepared to back into a site, insisting that turning is provided within the site. This can be difficult with sites for a small number of houses that have limited access provision. Here, a design that does not require a refuse vehicle to enter a site by erection of a bin store might be proposed. This may be complemented by smoke suppression systems fitted in the houses to satisfy the fire department in terms of access for fire equipment.

Sight lines

Sight lines are imaginary lines drawn from a position just into the egress from a site to allow drivers of emerging vehicles to see vehicles travelling along the road they are to emerge onto. It is clear that where traffic is likely to be travelling at speed it will be necessary to see it at a greater distance than if it is travelling more slowly.

There are two distances to consider with a sight line, the x-distance and the y-distance. The x-distance is the short distance from the kerb (the x-point) of the road into the site. The y-distance is the much longer line from the x-point to a point on the kerb that forms a triangle with a short height and a long base. The hypotenuse then is the sight line and visibility is available within the triangle. It would be of no effect if trees were to be planted within it.

Acoustic report

An acoustic report may need to be undertaken where a site is close to a noise source such as an aircraft flight path or a motorway. An acoustics surveyor will record and measure sound on site and make recommendations for insulating the structure against excess noise. This report will be submitted with the application.

Notification of owners

It is perhaps a curious aspect of a planning application process that the applicant does not require the permission of the owner of land to apply for planning permission to develop it and indeed they do not have to have any interest in the land to apply for planning permission on it. In *Hanily v Minister of Local Government and Planning* [1952] 1 All E.R. 1293 the High Court held that anyone who hoped to acquire an interest in the land could properly apply for planning permission. The developer merely has to serve notice on the owner that the application is made (see section 65 of the Town and Country Planning Act 1990).

In certain circumstances, if an application is made for planning permission on another's land, the applicant will be unpopular and will probably extract the comment that the owner would not sell the land in any event. I am not sure that this is always true. I am currently developing a site where my colleague made two such applications showing two alternative access points as both landowners had categorically refused to sell. The strategy relied on one of the owners agreeing a sale once planning had been granted and the 'money was on the table'. Once planning was granted, sure enough – these landowners raced to their telephones and a deal was concluded with one of them.

It is, of course, unlikely that an applicant will go to the expense of making a planning application on another's land without some form of interest or undertaking from the owner. The most common reason why an application is made on land not in the ownership of the applicant is that the land is not 'yet' in the ownership of the applicant. It is subject to an option or contract to purchase it subject to the grant of the planning application being applied for.

The LPA has a period of time to consider whether to grant or refuse to grant permission for the application. This period is eight weeks from the date the application is received (see Article 20 of the GPDO).

Fees
The LPA has the ability to charge a fee for the processing of any planning application pursuant to regulations made by the Secretary of State (section 303 Town and Country Planning Act 1990). Today this fee is collected online from the developer. Fees are calculated according to the scale of the application being made and the number of applications being made. Separate applications for discharge of conditions will see fees mount up.

Twin tracking
It is of course possible to submit more than one application for planning permission with some variations or modifications in the second one anticipating the views of the LPA. Why then do some developers submit two identical applications? This is known as 'twin tracking' and was used with more contentious applications that may take longer than the statutory eight weeks to decide. The idea is to appeal against non-determination of one of the applications following the eight-week period and to continue negotiating the other application. This is a strategy that relies on the likelihood of the planning inspector being more willing to grant permission than the LPA. It is in my view a strategy undertaken to intimidate the LPA and indeed LPAs are now able to refuse to accept applications that merely recite previous ones.

Determination of a planning application by the Local Planning Authority
The LPA may:

(a) grant planning permission either conditionally or subject to such conditions as they think fit; or

(b) refuse planning permission.

     (section 70(1) Town and Country Planning Act 1990).

In dealing with the application section 70(2) provides that the LPA 'shall have regard to the provisions of the development plan so far as material to the application, and to other material considerations'. Section 26 of the Planning and Compensation Act 1991 adds a provision to Part 2 of the 1990 Act that section 54A be added. It reads, 'Where in making determination under the planning acts, regard is to be had to the development plan, the determination shall be made in accordance with the plan unless material considerations indicate otherwise'. This provision has, however, been amended by the Planning and Compulsory Purchase Act 2004 at section 37(6). It introduces the word 'must' rather than 'shall'.

Material considerations
It will be seen then that departure from the development plan can be envisaged if material considerations indicate otherwise. What then might be a 'material consideration'? It appears that such considerations must be of a planning nature (see *Stringer v Minister of Housing and Local Government* [1970] 1 W.L.R. 1281). However, it seemed to Cooke J in that case that any consideration which relates to the use and development of land is capable of being a planning consideration.

Planning permission will append a summary of the reasons for the grant and where subject to conditions, reasons for the imposition of each condition imposed.

Delegation
LPAs are able to discharge their functions to a committee or an officer of the authority (section 101 Local Government Act 1972). All local authorities delegate planning functions to planning committees and often to planning officers. Indeed, figures show that the majority of planning decisions are made by officers without the need to be considered by the planning committee.

Planning permissions
Planning permissions will be issued by an LPA in writing setting out the description of the development including reference to submitted drawings and setting out the conditions that are to be satisfied to comply with the permission. These conditions may be those that need to be satisfied pre-commencement, pre-construction, pre-occupation or indeed during the course of construction.

Duration

Section 91 of the Town and Country Planning Act 1990 states that every planning permission granted or deemed to be granted shall be subject to the condition that the development permitted by it must be begun not later than five years beginning with the date on which it was granted or such period as directed by the planning authority. That period has now been reduced to three years by section 51 of the Planning and Compulsory Purchase Act 2004. If development is commenced after expiry then that development is not authorised by the permission.

The duration is different for outline planning permission whereby the expiry date is two years from approval of the final reserve matter provided that that application was submitted within three years of the outline approval.

Commencement

Section 56 of the Town and Country Planning Act 1990 prescribes the 'material operations' that constitute a 'start' of the development.

(a) Any work of construction in the course of erection of a building.

(b) Any work of demolition of a building.

(c) The digging of a trench that is to contain the foundations or part of the foundations of a building.

(d) Any operation in the course of laying out or constructing a road or part of a road.

(e) Any change of use of any land which constitutes material development.

It is important to note that the start will not be valid if it is not made pursuant to the permission. It is not acceptable to dig a trench that is not likely to contain the foundations of the development. Any demolition should be that granted in the planning permission. It seems that if the trench is backfilled for safety purposes then it is still a start (see the case of *High Peak BC v SSE* [1981] J.P.L. 366).

So too must the developer ensure that they have complied with the conditions to the planning consent in that they have been discharged by the LPA. Operations that contravene a planning permission will not start the development.

In *FG Whitley and Sons v SOS for Wales* [1990] J.P.L. 675, Woolf LJ stated:

> *'If the operations contravene the conditions they cannot properly be described as commencing the development authorised by the permission.'*

7.7 Conservation areas

Certain areas of the built environment are designated under section 69 Planning (Listed Buildings and Conservation Areas) Act 1990 as conservation areas. This designation is in recognition of the special architectural or historic quality the character or appearance of which it is desirable to preserve or enhance. It does not mean that no new development will ever take place in the conservation area. If a proposal is to demolish a less attractive building or extinguish an undesirable use, then a new development could potentially enhance the conservation area. However, any new development will be subject to stringent rules in respect to design and materials.

Trees in conservation areas are not necessarily given TPOs but they are given special protection. A written application for consent for the lopping or felling of trees in a conservation area is to be made six weeks prior to doing so. This gives the LPA an opportunity to serve a TPO. If they do not do so, then works can take place.

7.8 Listed buildings

Certain buildings are listed on a register prepared by DCMS as protected to preserve our cultural heritage. They are classed as Grade 1, Grade 2* and Grade 2. They can often be an important part of the appearance of towns and countryside.

Projects involving a listed building for restoration or conversion are usually only undertaken by developers with confidence, courage and knowledge as there are a great many restrictions to the alteration, renovation and repair of listed buildings.

Listed Building Consent

Listed Building Consent (LBC)(section 16 Planning (Listed Buildings and Conservation Areas) Act 1990) will be required to have been granted by the local planning authority in addition to any other planning permissions that might be required for the project. Such a consent cannot be granted in outline and therefore much detail will need to be put together as part of an application. The LBC, when granted, will contain a long list of conditions.

Listed building conditions

The conditions to an LBC will require much further work to be done. Reports from archaeologists, timber and damp reports, restoration brickwork, structural engineers' proposals, material samples and method statements from contractors will be needed.

It is important to appreciate the additional cost associated with the discharge of listed building consent conditions together with the additional time it may take to have the conditions discharged. These conditions will require the involvement of a number of consultants and specialist contractors. I refer later to VAT but it is perhaps worth mentioning at this point that any reduced VAT rate applicable to a restoration of a listed building from commercial use to residential use does not apply to professional fees. Architects and engineers employed on the project will charge VAT at the standard rate.

Design

The architect is the lead consultant and particularly so with work to a listed building. They may be required to draw up window schedules and timber schedules to determine what should remain in the building and what might be removed. They will be required to supervise the discharge of the listed building conditions. Sections of the building may have to be drawn up.

It is likely that an archaeology report will be required describing the building and what needs to be preserved.

Listed buildings are, more often than not, old and a structural engineer will need to assess the building and advise on any structural work that will need to take place.

Building regulations

It is unlikely that the renovation of a listed building and the preservation requirements will meet the building regulations required of a new build house. A compromise will be reached between the building inspector and the local authority to ensure that a robust approach is taken to building regulations while preserving essential elements of the listed building.

Restoration specialists

A listed building may well require timber and damp remediation work and a report will have to be prepared to show what work is required. Waterproofing of exposed walls is undertaken by fitting an inner skin to existing walls that allow a cavity to drain any water ingress to the exterior of the building.

Brickwork repair is a specialist task and will generally need to be documented in a report prepared by a restoration bricklayer. Steels will often be fitted to the structure replacing timbers. Restoration work to a listed building will then often require a great deal more consideration than new build work and should not be undertaken by those without experience.

7.9   Planning conditions

The grant of planning permission will be issued subject to conditions. Section 55 Town and Country Planning Act 1990 says that these are 'such conditions as the LPA deem fit'.

This general power is given in section 70(1) Town and Country Planning Act 1990.

In *Newbury DC v SSE* [1981] A.C. 578, the House of Lords considered the validity of a condition imposed under the general power. The House of Lords reached the conclusion that conditions must:

(a)   be imposed for a planning purpose and not an ulterior one;

(b)   fairly and reasonably relate to the development permitted;

(c)   not be so unreasonable that no reasonable authority could have imposed them.

Planning Circular 11/95 sets out a six fold test that conditions should meet. They must be necessary, relevant to planning, relevant to the development permitted, enforceable, precise and reasonable.

It is not acceptable for a planning authority to impose a condition to a planning permission that effectively discharges a duty of the authority on the developer (see *R v Hillingdon LBC Ex p Royco Homes Ltd* [1974] 1 Q.B. 720).

There must be a connection between the condition and the permission. A condition should not attempt to control something not created by the permitted development.

A condition can be void for uncertainty if it cannot be ascribed a meaning and it will be invalid if it is unenforceable.

Planning obligations

Planning obligations are described below at Paragraph 7.11 but it should be mentioned at this stage that the mechanism for obtaining the developer's consent to matters that would ordinarily contravene a condition is the section 106 planning obligation. This is a legal agreement entered into between the developer and the planning authority which places obligations on the developer that would be unenforceable as planning conditions.

7.10   Typical conditions

Again, I will assume a project: let's say four detached houses.

It is likely that a number of conditions will be listed on the planning permission and these should be read through carefully.

Planning permissions will always be issued subject to conditions. These conditions fall into four categories; those that need to be satisfied pre-commencement of the project, those that require to be satisfied pre-construction, those that require to be satisfied pre-occupation and those that need to be complied with during the construction process.

It is important to read through a copy of the planning permission and mark up the categories of conditions such that the team is aware which of them have to be satisfied pre-commencement, which need to be satisfied pre-construction, and perhaps less importantly those that need to be in place pre-occupation of the completed scheme.

It is therefore important to make all consultants aware of the timescale for satisfying planning conditions such that a start is not made on site with one vital condition remaining unsatisfied. Where conditions are fundamental to the grant of planning permission, the failure to satisfy them can result in the permission becoming invalid.

Pre-commencement conditions

Examples of pre-commencement conditions might be an environmental report or stipulations set out in the habitat report. These are perhaps the most important as failure to comply can invalidate the permission and the developer will presumably be keen to get started on the project.

Pre-construction conditions

An example of a pre-construction condition might be a written statement setting out the manner in which works on site will proceed.

Pre-occupation conditions
Pre-occupation conditions may require that car parking spaces are operational prior to occupation.

Conditions to be complied with during construction
Compliance conditions are merely those requirements which have to be adhered to during the construction process, for example, to erect a protective fence around a group of trees or to comply with set working hours. Clearly there is no need to obtain further consent to such conditions but it is as well to make sure that the site manager is fully aware of them.

I mark up a copy of the permission in my file highlighting the subject of the condition. In other words, if it refers to trees, I just highlight the word trees to save reading through the whole document time and again. This helps me when referring back to the document.

I then mark the conditions to fall in to each category:

• Commencement conditions

• Pre-construction conditions

• Pre-occupation conditions

• Finally, there are the compliance conditions.

Clearly it is important to first target the pre-commencement and pre-construction conditions in order to get started on site. Let us go over what these might be for a residential project.

Materials
The local authority planning officer will want to approve the materials to be used in construction.

Ecology
The planning authority will no doubt have required an ecology report with the planning application. The condition on the planning permission will refer to this report and the need to comply with it together, potentially, with any further reports that need to take place. Biodiversity net gain is the new requirement under the Environment Act 2021 that seeks to ensure that all new development creates some form of enhancement to biodiversity. This

is often created by the inclusion of bat boxes, natural open space areas and access holes in fences for small mammals.

Trees
The developer will no doubt have submitted a tree report and there is likely to be a condition referring to this report and requiring compliance with it.

Site management plan
The LPA may require approval of the site management plan. This will set out the location of cabins, storage, car parking and service trenches. The plan may refer to working hours, published local authority guidance, wheel washing, access and egress from the site and staffing. The plan can be written in a way that is of use to subcontractors making tenders for works. This plan is useful to fulfil the requirement of the principal designer in that it will plan the layout of the site during construction work to ensure a safe and secure environment.

7.11   Planning obligations and Community Infrastructure Levy
Community Infrastructure Levy
Many local planning authorities now charge a community infrastructure levy (CIL) ostensibly to meet the cost of infrastructure in their area. This is payable upon the implementation of planning permissions granted by them. The authority will have to have a charging schedule (section 211(1) Planning Act 2008) in place for this, setting out the charge for each additional square metre of gross internal floor space to be constructed. The developer, usually as part of the planning application, will notify the planning authority in standard form of CIL information and an assumption of liability setting out the names of those responsible for paying the charge when it becomes due. The grant of planning permission will then include a liability notice for CIL and a calculation of how much it is to be (Regulation 65 Community Infrastructure Regulations (2010)). Notice of commencement must be notified in standard form. It is not sufficient to notify by email (see *Shropshire Council v SSCLG* [2019] EWHC 16 (Admin)).

Section 106 planning agreements
The original purpose of a planning agreement was to secure, for the benefit of a development, such works that are deemed necessary to accommodate the development itself. These agreements under section 52 Town and Country Planning Act 1956 were to secure such works as the widening of the footway outside the site or the designation of an area within the site for wildlife or community use.

Section 52 was replaced in the consolidating Town and Country Planning Act 1990 by section 106 and the following year an addendum was made to the section that changed this to planning obligation agreements in the form of section 106. These should only be used where it is not possible to address unacceptable impacts through a planning condition.

Paragraph 56 of the National Planning Policy Framework states that section 106 agreements are to be:

(a)   necessary to make the development acceptable in planning terms;

(b)   directly related to the development; and

(c)   fairly and reasonably related in scale and kind to the development.

The agreement is made by deed and is registrable as a local land charge.

Why is it necessary to enter into a planning obligation agreement? Why not just condition the planning permission? Planning conditions have always been imposed to benefit the approved development which I understand to be the site within the boundary marked in red on the plans, whereas a planning obligation agreement can have wider implications.

Affordable housing requirements
Affordable housing is housing provided to those who cannot afford market housing and it is provided at a subsidised rent. Local authorities and housing associations are the providers of such housing and it is common for planning authorities to require an allocation of a number of homes to be built on certain sites to be for affordable housing.

Most LPAs will require a specified contribution of plots for affordable housing for schemes greater than a certain number of units. Say, for example, an LPA policy states that sites of more than 10 units must contribute 30% of units for affordable housing, then that requirement will need to be met. Some LPAs will require 50% of sites of over one dwelling. What then are the issues?

First, it is of course the land that the developer contributes, not the house itself or the building costs. They are still entitled to a building contract for the affordable element at a reasonable return.

It is usual for the LPA to require the developer to provide the affordable units to a registered provider on the LPA's list. The registered provider will be a housing association. They must, therefore, reach an agreement with the registered provider for the sale of the land to them and a building contract to construct the units for the registered provider.

They must build units that comply with housing association requirements or they will not be able to deliver them to a registered provider. This means that the developer will need to be careful not to undersize dwellings and to be mindful of specification requirements which will usually be seeking low cost maintenance.

Upon signing the agreement with the registered provider, the developer will of course have sold the affordable units. Therefore, there is often a cashflow benefit in providing affordable housing. Usually, payment will be made as the units are built, in stage payments. This sometimes contrasts favourably with the situation where the developer develops these houses for private sale with interest costs to a bank.

The developer has the opportunity to ensure at the design stage that the affordable housing occupies any less desirable locations on the site.

I repeat. It is always essential to ensure that Gross Internal Areas (GIAs) are as prescribed for affordable housing. Too small may disallow the registered provider from accepting them; too large will waste money as the developer will not be compensated. If someone is designing to the minimum requirement they must be sure that GIAs will not be reduced at working drawing stage by widening walls or accommodating fire regulations. The margin to be added to the construction contract price is up to 20%. This may seem high but consider that the developer has provided the site and taken the risk in securing the planning permission as well as paying for the fees incurred.

Some developers have become specialists at sourcing and developing sites specifically to meet the needs of registered providers and with that, gained expertise in the requirements. As can be seen above, selling to a registered provider has advantages. There are no interest charges to a bank or costs of sale to estate agents. Some registered providers pay good prices for accommodation particularly for shared ownership units where they themselves receive a higher return. Also, affordable housing may have lesser requirements for parking which may save space on a site.

Viability assessments for affordable housing

In some cases, it can be argued that it is not viable for a scheme to provide affordable housing. The scheme may be providing some alternative community facility such as a library or amenity space. In other cases, the existing use value of the site is at a level that makes the allocation of part of the site for affordable housing questionable and in such cases a viability assessment undertaken by a specialist chartered surveyor is undertaken that may reduce the amount of affordable housing or eliminate the requirement altogether. If a developer has overpaid for a site, however, that does not make them free from an affordable housing contribution. For example, where the local plan made clear the requirement exists for a specific percentage of affordable housing, the fact that the developer did not take this into account when buying the site is not relevant to the viability assessment (see *Parkhurst Road Ltd v SSLG & Anor* [2018] EWHC 991 (Admin)).

7.12   Planning appeals

An appeal against the refusal by the local planning authority to grant planning permission is made to the Department of the Environment (section 78 Town and Country Planning Act 1990). The department will appoint an inspector to conduct the appeal and to issue a decision whether to allow it and grant planning permission or to agree with the LPA and refuse to grant permission.

The appeal process takes time, and the amount of time will depend on the procedure selected for the appeal. There are three procedures for appeal that can be adopted. First, for large scale developments a public inquiry may be pursued. This procedure requires expert witnesses, counsel and a great deal of money. It is unlikely that small developments will require this route.

Secondly, an appeal by written representation requires written statements from each side setting out their arguments for and against the proposal. As I write, I am advised that a written representation appeal can take six months to reach a decision.

Thirdly, an informal hearing is another process, somewhat less formal than a public inquiry but allows representation in front of an inspector which the appellant may wish to achieve.

The developer may conduct the appeal process themselves although it is more usual to instruct a planning professional to do so. The planner will be aware of similar cases and advise on the likelihood of success. I have undertaken many planning appeals, however, and have come to the conclusion that you really cannot predict an outcome.

My policy is to sail with the tide whenever possible. The developer should listen to the local planning officer and however much they disagree with the planning officer's analysis of the proposals, should consider carefully the prospect of a successful appeal outcome if the application contradicts the planning officer.

This is quite different from appealing against a refusal from a belligerent planning committee following the planner's recommendation for approval. Here one can often be more certain of a positive outcome. Even in these circumstances, however, it may be better to seek a compromise where one is available rather than the uncertainty of a planning appeal.

Judicial review
This is the process whereby certain interested parties have the right to apply to court to have the planning permission set aside where certain legal strictures were not observed. Such parties must have locus standi which simply means that they must have some form of vested interest in the outcome of the proceedings. In the case of *R v Swale Borough Council, ex parte Royal Society for the Protection of Birds* [1991] J.P.L. 39, the Royal Society for the Protection of Birds were acknowledged to have locus standi in relation to a proposal to develop a wet land in north Kent. In other words, they clearly had a relevant interest in the proposal.

Enforcement
Enforcement is the term used where the LPA wish to rectify a breach of planning control. Clearly, where a house has been built without planning permission and where planning permission would not have been granted, the LPA will be likely to enforce compliance with planning control which could mean demolition of the house altogether. More often the contravention is less drastic, and the enforcement notice may only require an adaption to the structure or occupation of the house.

Stop notices
A stop notice issued by an LPA is literally a requirement to stop work on a development. Such notices are rarely issued as first an enforcement notice will have been issued and compliance already secured, and under section 186 Town and Country Planning Act 1990, the LPA will be liable to pay compensation to the developer if the stop notice is quashed.

Case Study 5
Planning
Key issue. Establishing the right mix of units.

Developers will no doubt consider they have the right to formulate the mix of accommodation within a proposed development project with perhaps input from a local estate agent. In certain circumstances they would be mistaken. On two separate occasions in Royal Tunbridge Wells I was confronted with the planning authority's policy to provide a mix of accommodation on residential sites. I had thought this a worthy aspiration on large development sites but for a scheme of seven flats it seemed unnecessary. A long dialogue took place with planners in which my team tried to promote a scheme for 2-bedroom flats. In the end we had to settle for a mix of units from one large 3-bedroom flat to a tiny 1-bedroom flat which we were unhappy with. We sold the site on.

Some years later I purchased a site in Cranbrook within the Royal Tunbridge Wells borough. The site had had a variety of failed planning attempts and I resolved to seek the planners' views as to the mix of units to be provided. As predicted they sought units of 1 bedroom, 2 bedrooms and 3 bedrooms. Our planning application was approved on this basis.

The lesson you learn from this is perhaps that it is better to 'go with the tide' in such circumstances rather than fight adopted policy.

Case study 6
Refusal of grant of planning permission for proposed scheme
Key issue: Whether an appeal under section 78 Town and Country Planning Act 1990 is likely to be successful or whether it may make any subsequent dialogue with the LPA more difficult.

It is often the case that it is the refusal of planning permission for a project that has the developer seeking professional planning advice and many would say that they should have made their consultations when drawing up plans. A planning appeal can be an expensive undertaking and it is well worth the developer considering very carefully their chances of success. They will be well advised to consult with a professional planner who might be asked not only to advise the chance of success of any appeal but what further application to the LPA might meet with approval.

Over the years I have been in business I have seen many appeal decisions that do not seem to me to make sense. That I suppose is inevitable. The Inspector will be making a subjective judgement be it based on evidence, but what evidence are they to give the greater weight? It is almost impossible to predict the outcome of an appeal and advice I have had from leading planners has often, frankly, been wrong.

One potential outcome to an unsuccessful planning appeal is where an inspector not only refuses to allow the appeal but refers to something that is likely to confound any further application for development of the site. I had this on a small site where I was proposing demolition of a single house and the erection of three terraced houses. The planning authority refused the application on density grounds, but the Inspector, while agreeing with the planning authority, drew attention to the side wall of the adjoining building which stood forward of the existing house but would be at the same building line as the terrace proposed. This wall was flint and the Inspector held that it was a visible and attractive feature that should be retained whereas the proposed terrace would screen it. It was, by that comment, impossible to return to the LPA with revised proposals for a less dense development.

A similar outcome was where my company submitted a proposal for a sizable development of luxury flats in an attractive village. The logic as ever was the housing need and the requirement to build more new homes. The principle of development of the site was the subject of the debate with planners ending in a refusal to grant planning permission at first instance. The proposal, however, required the demolition of four rather run down Victorian houses and the Inspector, in dismissing the appeal, referred to the quality of the houses on the site and questioned their demolition. Again, it became very difficult to return to the LPA with proposals that would involve demolition of the existing houses.

What this teaches us that, notwithstanding the reasons for refusal, inspectors can occasionally introduce further reasons often merely by implication, making any subsequent application easier for the LPA to resist.

Chapter 8

Project planning

'By failing to prepare, you are preparing to fail.'
Benjamin Franklin

A residential development project will require expertise from a large number of consultants and specialists even before a spade is put in the ground. The developer will need to instruct the right professional team with the right experience and qualifications. That means telling them, in writing, precisely what they want them to do. It is no good saying later that they had not realised that an engineer would not be responsible for checking the timber frame loadings or learning that the architect did not design the staircase that has failed to fit. The developer should be clear and comprehensive in their instructions and put them in writing in a letter of engagement and have a copy signed by the consultant. The developer will need this documentation if they are to arrange collateral warranties for a funder as a comprehensive instruction is likely to be part of the funding requirements.

8.1   Pre-contract report
It is useful to prepare a pre-contract report at an early stage collating as much information as possible to circulate to the professional team. The report will describe the due diligence undertaken and identify the issues and abnormal costs in carrying out the scheme and identify issues that require to be resolved. The professional team will identify for themselves how they can contribute to resolution of these issues.

I like to collate as much information into the pre-contract report so that I know I can go to one place to retrieve information.

The report might take the following format:

Title name of site showing the postcode and any alternative names used. It is often the case that 'Land to rear of Whitehouse Lane' changes name when access is taken from Blackbrook Lane.

Date. This is a document that will be updated as progress is made so it is particularly important to show the date.

General description to give the reader an idea of what type of site they are being asked to work on. What shape is it, what is the area of the site, what are the levels and what is the location? Are there any existing buildings and will they be demolished or retained? If they are to be retained, are they listed and have they been subject to a structural inspection?

The report should consider the surrounding buildings, their use and intensification of use, access, age, any rights including rights of light and access they might claim over the site and any party walls. It should establish that the site has access from a public adopted highway or that it enjoys rights along the entire length of the road leading to the public highway. A ransom strip is accurately named where a developer is forced to negotiate access over someone else's land.

The report should give an idea as to any likely issues with sight lines so that these might be checked. Sometimes additional land will need to be acquired for sight lines to ensure that sufficient vision is available over the frontages of adjoining land. Include comments on any level changes at the access that may make works difficult or may inhibit access.

The report should record the name and address of the local planning authority along with a telephone number and names of any contacts made with the planning authority.

It should set out the results of any initial enquiries made and any planning policies that will affect the proposals for the project. If there are relevant extant or historic planning permissions these should be recorded in the report.

Information on any tree preservation orders relevant to the site or planning policies relating to the retention of trees should be recorded.

If a sketch layout plan outlining proposals has been prepared this could be attached to the report.

Title documents can be obtained from the land registry. A land registry plan should be attached to the report so that this can be checked to agree with the site survey. If there are any restrictive covenants in the charges register it is a good idea to record them here.

The developer should check the title to see that easements can be relied upon such as are noted in the property register. Will fresh easements or alteration of routes be required? If so, these may have to be negotiated with adjoining landowners.

Occupation of the site will need to be recorded including details of any leases, adverse possession issues and potential overriding interests.

If matters have progressed with the negotiation to purchase, the developer may wish to record in the report the terms and conditions of contracts or options that have been agreed with vendors. Timescales will be particularly important.

Information on existing drainage will be useful for the team so that they can consider new routes and connections, for example, the location of existing surface water and foul sewers, their capacities, depth of inverts and of course confirmation as to their adoption. This has become less of an issue since 1 October 2011 where shared drains and drains running under land owned by third parties become lateral drains under the private sewers transfer regulations.

Ground conditions will be checked by the environmental surveyor but a general comment as to subsoil obtained from local records might give an idea to the team as to the type of foundation that will be required. The use of the site may give an idea of soil contamination. The developer should always check the site and surrounds for Japanese knotweed. It can be very expensive to eradicate.

Inspection of a site should alert the developer to abnormal costs. Is there a large amount of demolition? Is there much concrete to break out? Will there be costs external to the site itself? Does the ground slope and what type of plants are growing on it? Comments as to these will be useful.

It is useful to provide a full report recording as much detail as has been able to establish at this stage so that the professional team are alerted to any specific action they need to take in the undertaking of their work. The report should include all information, for example postcodes. In this way it can be a point of reference saving time searching other documents for information.

Viewing arrangements, names and contact details are essential as clearly the team needs to be advised as to whom to contact to view the site.

8.2 Neighbours

It is unusual to complete the purchase of a site without having spoken to its neighbours. The development may have had to acquire something from them; a piece of the site, a sight line across the frontage of their property or an easement for drainage. A planning application will have been submitted and it is indeed rare for there to be no objection to proposals. What we have to consider is the rights that neighbours may have in some way to object, amend or proscribe the proposed development.

8.3 Boundaries

It is always desirable to know exactly where the boundaries of the site are. That means having a topographical survey undertaken and scrupulously comparing this with the registered title to the site. This can be done with a light test, i.e. one plan over the other at the same scale if there is some doubt about boundaries. In my experience neighbours can have expectations regarding the line of boundaries that do not align with title plans.

8.4 Party walls

Where construction is potentially liable to affect a wall of a neighbouring building or a wall owned jointly with a neighbouring property, there may be an obligation on the developer to engage a party wall surveyor to obtain agreement to construction proposals. Party walls used to exist only in cities – now they are nationwide. That is to say that the Party Wall Act 1996 sets out what party walls are and if a project is for construction or excavation within a certain distance of the neighbouring construction then the developer will need to serve a party wall notice.

The distances are set out in the Party Wall Act 1996 to be within three metres of the neighbouring wall where the excavation is to be taken below the foundation and within six metres where a line is drawn at a 45 degree angle from the base of the neighbouring foundation to the base of the proposed excavation.

8.5 Registered land

Since the Land Registration Act 2002 (section 4) all freehold land and leases over seven years transferred or granted in England have to be registered following transfer if they are not already. Failure to register would result in equitable ownership.

8.6 Unregistered land

Unregistered land is simply land that has not been registered at the Land Registry. This is presumably because it has not been transferred since compulsory registration, thus it remains in the same ownership and unregistered. The Land Registry does, however, encourage the registration of land and it is not necessary for a transfer to take place to secure registration.

8.7   Insurances
The project will need to be insured under several headings. I list these as follows:

(1)   The contractor's all risk insurance policy covering public liability, employees and the work being undertaken for the project. This is generally an annual policy taken out by the building contractor.

(2)   Any existing building or buildings. This insures any damage to these and is generally a property policy for a reinstatement cost.

(3)   Professional indemnity (PI) insurance where the contractor or developer is undertaking design, for example work is taking place under a design build contract, or as principal designer.

(4)   The PI insurances of the team professionals.

(5)   The insurances of subcontractors and suppliers.

(6)   Structural new home warranty.

(7)   Bonds and guarantees for highway or off site drainage works.

(8)   Property insurance for completed dwellings post the issue of practical completion certificates.

8.8   Appointing a team of professionals
A residential development project will require input from a team of professionals each playing an important part in its planning and implementation. The developer should be sure to appoint the professional team with clear instructions so that no part of the project is omitted and neither is there any misunderstanding as to who is responsible for each task. It is therefore useful to prepare a team list of the professionals as soon as these appointments have been made.

Team list

The team list should give contact details of the professionals engaged for the project. These may include an architect, civil and structural engineers, landscape architect, quantity surveyor, project manager, principal designer, new home warrantor, contractor, land surveyor, hydrologist, arboriculturist, ecologist, SAP architect, building control surveyor, soils and environmental surveyors, M&E engineers and a lawyer.

This is not a list of subcontractors. The appointment of subcontractors will come later in the project in the procurement process when quotations for works are being considered. Once terms are agreed with professional consultants and appointments are made, the team list can be circulated to all of them. The team list will allow professionals to contact each other for plans and specifications. This communication will assist the principal designer in their role of ensuring all design elements are communicated and understood and taken into account by all team members to avoid omissions and misunderstandings. The principal designer will ensure that the consultants' professional indemnity insurances are collated and retained on file for insurance purposes. Members of the team will communicate with each other, check and question information and notify alterations and updates to the project manager.

Let us then consider the team list and see who does what.

Architect

The architect will design the scheme and prepare site plans, floor plans, elevations and sections to obtain planning permission for the houses to be built. Upon grant of planning permission they will prepare working drawings and specifications for engineers and subcontractors. They will show the estate road where required for later detail by the civil engineer and may also help with plans such as transfer plans for sales and registration at the Land Registry and plans for services within the dwellings showing positions of power points and radiators.

Landscape architect

The landscape architect may mark up a landscape plan showing hard and soft landscaping detailing plants and providing a guide for their maintenance. On simple schemes the architect may incorporate this on their site plan and this is often enough to satisfy the landscape condition.

Structural engineer

The plans prepared by the architect will be submitted to the structural engineer so that they can calculate loadings and identify requirements for steels and padstones and prepare sub-structure drawings. They will analyse ground levels to see what retaining walls might need to be constructed and if of a certain height, will draw up structural drawings for these.

Civil engineer

The civil engineer will be responsible for foul and surface water drainage, estate roads and hard landscaping. They should notify the drainage authority of connection to the public sewer and obtain consent for this. This is the section 106 agreement under the Water Industries Act 1990.

Mechanical and electrical engineer

An M&E engineer is not always vital to the team. That is not to say that they do not make a valuable contribution but for a smaller project the idea of involving one additional member of the team to draw up service drawings may not seem necessary. Where they are engaged they will prepare the mechanical and electrical drawings and arrange the services to the site. They may also be responsible for preparing energy performance information at the end of the project.

Building inspector

Building inspectors used to be employed by local authorities' building control departments to ensure that buildings meet the building regulations. Today they are Approved Inspectors (AIs) qualified to undertake building control work in accordance with section 49 of the Building Act 1984 and the building approved inspectors regulations, and they are often privately owned firms of chartered surveyors. It is sometimes useful to allow the new home warrantor to select their preferred building inspector to avoid duplication of inspections. Alternatively, some local authorities still retain building control departments often working for several adjoining local authorities.

Quantity surveyor

Quantity surveyors prepare cost schedules for construction projects. They are not always required on smaller residential projects where experienced developers can use historic building cost information to produce cost schedules.

Party wall surveyor

A party wall surveyor will set out the works to be undertaken and serve notice on the adjoining owner. The adjoining owner may then agree to the works or appoint their own party wall surveyor to agree to the works. If there is any dispute between them a third surveyor will be appointed to decide the appropriate course of action. Party wall chartered surveyors are often members of the Pyramus and Thisbe club which is a learned society that deals solely with party wall matters and thereby its members are experts in this field.

Land surveyor
The land surveyor will prepare the topographical survey of the site recording buildings, levels and features. This is a most useful survey as it may reveal discrepancies with title plans. It will provide the architect with a scale plan upon which to base their site layout and the engineer with levels for them to make their recommendations. The land surveyor may return to site just prior to foundation construction to set out the works.

Environmental surveyor
A soils survey may need to be undertaken to ascertain ground conditions for foundation design and to establish whether there is contamination of soil. The environmental survey employs a rig to drill down into the substructure to collect samples for testing. Where the site has been used for industrial purposes it will be important to have soil samples analysed and it should be appreciated that where there has been contamination soils will need to be removed. This will incur a significant cost.

New home warrantor
A New Home Warranty is issued by an insurance company and is a warranty against financial loss incurred from structural failure of a new home. Most such warranties offer a remedial period of two years from legal completion of a house where minor faults are remedied at no cost to the buyer and a period of ten years structural guarantee. The National House Building Council (NHBC) was at one time the only body to issue such warranties but today there are a number of insurers in the market, many of whom are retail businesses reinsuring in the insurance markets. The new home warrantor is responsible for ensuring that the housebuilder has a new homes code in place such that the buyer is clear about such matters as service routes, suppliers, operational procedures for fittings and contact numbers for maintenance.

Ecologist
An ecology survey and report is often a requirement of a planning application. Such a report will make recommendations which are often recited or referred to in a planning condition attached to a planning permission. Many species of wildlife are protected under the Wildlife and Countryside Act 1981

sections 1 to 27 which is regulated by Natural England from whom licences have to be obtained when developments may affect wildlife habitats. In view of the sensitivity of timing of studies on site, an ecology survey can take a considerable time to prepare. The first requirement is the provisional ecology assessment in which the wildlife to be studied is identified. Clearly this should be sought early in the project planning as in some cases the viability of the project may be called into question by the result.

SAPs assessor

A Standard Assessment Procedure (SAP) is undertaken in accordance with Part L of the Building Regulations which is concerned with energy efficiency. A new home has to comply with SAP ratings which are required to produce an Energy Performance Certificate (EPC). It is usual to submit drawings to a SAP specialist at design stage so that they can advise whether modifications will need to be made prior to construction. The SAP specialist will measure the area of the proposed building, examine the specification of materials and the energy consumption of the heating system, lighting, ventilation and renewable technologies. This information will be uploaded to software to produce a Target Emission Rate (TER). Upon completion of the building a further examination of the new home will take place including an air test and the information submitted to the building inspector for them to issue the final certificate.

Hydrologist

With flooding an increasing concern, it is important to ensure that the site drains well and that buildings are constructed with sufficient raised floor levels such that any flooding does not affect occupants. This is easier to achieve with new homes as it often simply means raising a floor level but it can be an issue with renovations.

Acoustics consultant

Acoustics consultants will specify materials and design of exterior walls, floors and roofs to mitigate noise and vibration from external sources such as flight paths, motorways and underground railway tunnels. Sound transmission, whether airborne or impact sound, is covered by Part E of the Building Regulations and therefore dealt with by the architect in their design and specification.

Health and safety consultant

Building sites have to comply with the Construction (Design and Management) Regulations 2015 (CDM Regulations) and there are a number of documents that will be kept on site to evidence the adherence to health and safety. The health and safety consultant will make frequent visits to the site to ensure that procedures for health and safety are being followed and that all required documentation is maintained on site. The appointment of a health and safety consultant is for the developer to decide. Failure to comply with a health and safety regime may result in a visit from the health and safety inspector and closure of the site, as well as, of course, risking the safety of operatives on site.

Arboriculturist
Many local planning authorities will insist on a tree survey as part of the planning application. Preserving trees is important for the environment. A professional arboriculturist will need to provide a report as to root protection and measures for crown lifting and pruning which can be quite complex.

Principal designer
The principal designer is a role created by the CDM Regulations 2015. By designer, it does not mean that they design anything. It simply means that they are responsible for sorting out communication between design parties and safety of design and the recording of this information. Often this role is undertaken by the architect but it can be a specialist or another professional. There are many people involved in the construction team. Communication affects so many aspects: design, deliveries, specification, site rules and procedures. When something goes wrong someone will say, 'I didn't know'. Communication is essential to avoid mistakes and to avoid injury.

I always say the person in the driving seat is best suited to the role of principal designer. The driver of a car does not pass responsibility to their passenger for any accidents that may occur. If they attempted to do so, the passenger might say, 'OK but I need to take out insurance and make up a report on your driving and the condition of the car. For this I will charge you £5,000'. This would be a reasonable response. Better in my view for the project manager or developer who has instigated and overseen the project to undertake the role of principal designer. They are in any event responsible and will be in touch with all aspects of the project.

8.9   Letters of engagement
The letter of engagement is the instruction to the consultant setting out the scope of the work required of them and confirming the fee structure agreed. This letter should be retained and should the consultant be required to give a collateral warranty it will be specified in the agreement together with a requirement for a copy of professional indemnity insurance.

The developer should not be tempted to save money by engaging unqualified 'professionals'. Not only can this lead to issues and omissions but it may not actually save money. Banks, insurance companies, surveyors and lawyers will wish to see that the professional who has been appointed is properly qualified for the job to reduce the risk of something going wrong. They will also wish to see that professionals are well covered for any design errors by suitable and adequate professional indemnity insurance should something actually go wrong.

8.10   Professional indemnity insurance

All professionals are required to have professional indemnity (PI) insurance and a developer is running a huge risk if they engage professionals without it. In fact, they may find it difficult or expensive to obtain new homes warranty insurance or finance if they do not have PI insurance. The requirement is for those with a design input to be insured. This clearly includes architects and engineers but also piling contractors, timber frame contractors and suppliers of precast floor beams. The developer should ask for a copy of their insurance and keep it on file.

I heard of a new homes warrantor charging a huge indemnity premium precisely because members of the technical team the developer had assembled were unqualified. The warrantor had priced the risk.

When seeking a quotation from a professional consultant the developer should state the requirement for the consultant to sign a collateral warranty as part of the terms of appointment which itself should be set out in writing and signed by the consultant. This may save prevarications later when seeking to return the signed collateral warranties to the funding bank.

8.11   Services to the construction site

Prior to commencement of works services will need to be disconnected and temporary supplies of water and electricity will need to be put in place. This can be a time consuming process and construction work cannot commence without water and electricity. It is important to arrange disconnections and temporary supplies as soon as possible.

If the site is vacant the developer might agree with the vendor for them to apply for disconnections before legal completion of the purchase and while the site remains in their ownership to save time.

8.12 Road agreements

New estate roads and their associated drainage have long been considered for adoption by the local authority. An estate road design is submitted for adoption under section 38 of the Highways Act 1980. The section 38 agreement is made between the developer and the highway authority. It is usual for a developer to pay a bond to the highway authority to ensure that works are carried out as specified and remedial work is undertaken following a maintenance period. The bond is refunded after this period.

Unadopted roads

Where a new road is being constructed which is to remain privately owned by perhaps a management company owned by the residents of the houses to be constructed, no section 38 agreement will need to be entered into. The developer should be aware that under section 33 of the Local Government (Miscellaneous Provisions) Act 1982 it is possible for a highway authority to require an advanced payment for works that may occur should they adopt a private road in future. This is a rare requirement, however.

Bonds and guarantees

Works to existing highways will require a licence and a payment of a bond to the highway authority (section 50 New Roads and Street Works Act 1991). The bond is held by the highway authority for a period of time in order to compensate for any remedial works that need to be undertaken over a given period (usually three years). Highway works of this kind will include connection to foul and surface water sewers in the highway.

Insurance indemnities

It is possible for a developer to pay an insurance premium rather than lodge a bond with the highway authority. This gives the benefit of payment of a lesser amount than the bond itself by way of a single premium. At the time of writing such insurance is expensive and the lodgement of a bond may well be the better option.

California Bearing Ratio (CBR) tests

The California Bearing Ratio is the ratio of force required per unit area that is needed to penetrate the soil mass. The CBR test was developed by the California highway authority to evaluate the bearing capacity of sub-grade soil. It is therefore used for foundation design of new estate roads.

Crossover licences

This is the licence granted by the highway authority to allow a developer to lower the kerb and tarmac the footpath surface to give access to the development. It is granted in accordance with section 274 Highways Act 1980 and may be referred to as a section 274 agreement.

If access to the development crosses the footway from a highway, it will need the permission of the highway authority to construct a crossover. The highway authority will insist that only its approved contractor can undertake this work, notwithstanding any very capable ground worker on site. It is unlikely that the highway authority will refuse to grant permission for this as there will be planning permission but a crossover licence will be required as the estate road is entering the highway. This application will need to be made as soon as possible and the developer should be prepared to undertake the work as there will be time limits from grant of the licence to implementation of the works. What must be avoided is leaving this too late in the project as the highway authority does not regard this as high priority. It is aggravating to have a sale ready to complete and to be awaiting a crossover licence.

Agreements for undertaking street works

Connection to sewers in the highway outside the site will require a license under section 50 New Roads and Street Works Act 1991. Application for this licence has to be made to the local highway authority. A refundable bond will be required in order to obtain the licence and in addition the applicant will be required to supply a detailed design drawing clearly showing the proposed area of excavation, and a traffic management drawing with dimensions showing how traffic, including pedestrians, will be directed. Also, accreditation details of the supervisor responsible for the works should be supplied. Failure to comply with these requirements is a criminal offence.

Closure of highways

Often, works within the highway do not warrant its closure. If vehicles can pass the works, it is as well to try to avoid closure. Closure will require a traffic plan and diversion signage together with a strict timescale of works. Any extension of the timescale of works will often incur a financial penalty.

Closure of footpaths

If there is a public footpath crossing the site, it will generally have to be maintained as it is a public right of way unless the project involves building over the footpath and it is necessary to apply for its closure. Closure can be made by application to the county council under section 257 and section 261

Town and Country Planning Act 1990 but generally an alternative route will need to be proposed and a fee will be payable. If it is necessary to undertake works such as groundworks where excavation across the footpath is necessary, a temporary closure by order application can be made under section 14 Road Traffic Regulation Act 1984. This closure will be limited to a period of six months unless a further period is approved by the Secretary of State.

8.13   Drainage adoption agreements
Adoption of new sewers is made under section 104 Water Industry Act 1991.

Drainage from the site, both foul and surface water, will generally need to connect to a public sewer. The alternative would be to drain surface water by soakaways or perhaps to a stream, and foul into a septic tank system. A drain serves one building or curtilage whereas a sewer is designed to serve more than one. It is often the case that drains do not connect direct to a public sewer. They may connect to a drain on neighbouring property pursuant to an existing easement. One may have negotiated an easement to connect one's drain to a drain on neighbouring property. In cases such as this, drains are subject to rules introduced on 1 October 2011 whereby shared drains become lateral drains and a drain from one property running under the land of another is a lateral drain. These become adopted by the drainage authority which means that the responsibility for their maintenance lies with the drainage authority.

8.14   Demolition
Demolition of existing residential buildings generally requires planning permission. If the planning permission for the project reads, 'Demolition of and construction of' then the planning permission will be in place for the demolition.

There is also a requirement to give notice of the demolition to the local authority under section 81 Building Act 1984. Generally, the demolition contractor will do this.

Once again, I suggest that all this information – reports, plans, approvals, minutes and agreements – be filed on a cloud system for ease of reference and retrieval.

Case study 7
Requirement of consent for development proposals
Key issue: Scheme of management under section 19 Leasehold Reform Act 1967.

Facts of the case study
The developer had assembled a site for redevelopment. The existing use of the land was as five separate dwellings together with two additional parcels of land used as car parking. The houses on the site had been held on long leases from the Dulwich estate and at various times since 1967, all five lessees exercised their right to enfranchise pursuant to the provisions of section 1 Leasehold Reform Act 1967. Of the two remaining parcels, one was held by the Dulwich estate although used by the owners of the houses. It is assumed that this was not, at the time of enfranchisement, deemed land appurtenant to any of the houses. The car park area was to the rear and part of a police station.

The site thus assembled was considered suitable for a development of 15 terraced houses and garages and parking set around a mews style courtyard. Communal areas of land including landscaped areas, driveway and forecourts and pathways were to be held by a residents' association company with covenants between each house owner and the association regulating the maintenance, repair and decoration of the estate.

Planning permission for the development was granted by London Borough of Southwark without any recourse being made to the developer for amendments to be made to submitted plans.

Subsequent to the planning permission, an application was made to the Dulwich estate for permission to implement planning permission due to its scheme of management under section 19. The estate appointed an architect to advise it on the design and a surveyor to undertake negotiation with the developer.

Plans were refused by the Dulwich estate due to density and design. Further consultations took place between the developer and the estate's surveyor which resulted in the modification of the scheme including the reduction of the number of houses to 14.

Analysis of legal issues

The scheme of management had been validly approved and applied to the Dulwich estate where enfranchisement of estate properties had taken place subject to section 1 Leasehold Reform Act 1967.

Property within the geographical boundaries of the estate excluded from the scheme of management was limited to that acquired by compulsory purchase order prior to 1967 and such properties were referred to as 'alien freehold'. The land to the rear of the police station was just such alien freehold. The scheme of management did not therefore apply to that part of the development or the police station land.

The development control criteria of the Dulwich estate had been far more rigorous than that of London Borough of Southwark planning authority. The private planning control vested in the Dulwich estate was more effective in development control than were the public controls of the LPA.

The estate's scheme of management did not apply to the alien freehold and thus it was only subject to the consent of the LPA.

The scheme of management set up pursuant to the Leasehold Reform Act 1967 had given the Dulwich estate formidable power to limit development. Any appeal against the estate's decision was limited to arbitration to decide whether the estate 'withheld consent arbitrarily'. An illustration of arbitration was given in *Estate Governors of Alleyn's College of God's Gift at Dulwich v Williams* [1994] 23 E.G. 127.

Sir Donald Nicolls said that, 'A statutory pre-requisite to the making of a scheme was a certificate from the minister to the effect that in order to maintain adequate standards of appearance and amenity and regulate redevelopment in the area in event of tenants acquiring the landlord's interest in their house and premises under the act, it was the minister's opinion likely to be the general interest that the landlord should retain powers of management in respect of enfranchised property.'

Clause 15 of the scheme gave the estate governors freedom to give or withhold their consent. However, they may withhold their consent only if to do so would, in all circumstances, be reasonable. In section 19 Landlord and Tenant Act 1927 such consent 'shall not be unreasonably withheld'. Then there is the test of reasonableness applicable to statutory authorities expressed in *Associated Provincial Picture Houses v Wednesbury Corporation* [1948] 1 K.B.

223 which examines whether a decision is perverse such as no reasonable authority would have come to it.

The issue in *Williams* was therefore not one of whether consent should or should not have been given but whether the estate governors acted reasonably in refusing consent. The matter was referred to further arbitration.

Conclusion

This case study illustrates the powers of administrators of schemes of management under the Leasehold Reform Act 1967 and now under Chapter 4 section 69 Leasehold Reform Housing and Urban Renewal Act 1993. Examination of the *Williams* case reveals that governors have to act reasonably but there is less opportunity for a successful appeal in the way there is against a refusal of planning permission. The developer must be aware of the existence of a potential for restriction.

Chapter 9

Building regulations

'An habitation giddy and unsure Hath he that buildeth on a vulgar heart.' (Henry 4ᵗʰ part 2)
Shakespeare

Those who would cut corners for a quick gain were always prone to an unsuccessful outcome. Today builders have more than just their conscience to comply with. Residential buildings have to comply with a list of building regulations made pursuant to the Building Act 1984 that allows the Secretary of State to make regulations to ensure safety, energy efficiency, prevention of waste and contamination of water. The regulations are a set of Approved Documents referred to as Parts A to R that give standards for the design and construction of buildings including: Structure (Part A), Drains (Part H), Ventilation (Part F) etc. A local authority is responsible for the enforcement of building regulations but in practice approved inspectors will be appointed to ensure that standards are met.

9.1   Approved Inspectors

Today, approved building inspectors (AIs) are not only those working for local authorities but private firms of chartered surveyors too, pursuant to section 49 Building Act 1994 and Building (Approved Inspectors etc.) Regulations 2010. It is therefore possible to appoint just one inspector for both building regulations and new homes warranty inspections.

The AI's inspections of the works are usually approval of plans and working drawings. The first task is for them to issue an initial notice to the local authority (section 47 Building Act 1984) with details of the developer, the location of the site and the use of the proposal.

The AI will be responsible for inspection, issuing the initial notice to the local authority, awareness of ground conditions and approval of foundations and ground floor slabs, any gas membranes, soil pipes, inspection and approval of roof structure and then final inspection. The new homes warranty inspections may add further inspections or verifications depending on the requirements of the warrantor. The AI will prepare a report following each inspection and a copy will be sent to site, listing any remedial work to be undertaken.

9.2 Requirements to secure the final certificate

The final certificate is issued by the AI upon inspection of the building and certification upon practical completion. It is therefore necessary for the developer to ensure that regulations have been satisfied and that certificates have been issued where required (as follows) in order to secure the final certificate.

SAPs

The Standard Assessment Procedure is the recommended methodology for measuring the energy rating of residential dwellings. It is a calculation of the annual energy costs for space heating, water heating and lighting. The SAP rating is a scale from 1 to 100. These ratings form the basis of satisfying Approved Document L (Conservation of fuel and power) and will be used to complete an Energy Performance Certificate (EPC) upon practical completion.

Air leakage tests

Air leakage can occur through gaps and cracks in the building fabric, often caused by service runs so are not necessarily visible. Air tests are therefore carried out to confirm compliance with Approved Document L. For residential developments, a representative sample of the houses is generally acceptable for testing.

Mastic sealants are used to close cracks and gaps in the fabric and are used internally and externally to fill unsightly cracks around sanitaryware, skirtings and windows.

Gas Safe Certificate

The Gas Safe Register is the official registration body in the UK to protect the public from unsafe gas work. All gas engineers need to be registered and new dwellings are issued with a Gas Safe Certificate on completion of gas works.

Electrical certificate

A certificate of compliance for electrical installation is issued by the electrician on completion of the works.

Fire safety report

A fire safety report is undertaken by a fire expert when there is a communal area such as a staircase in a block of flats. It is usual to equip such an area with a fire detection and alarm system together with a smoke ventilation system to ensure the staircase remains free from smoke in the event of a fire. An installation certificate will be required for release of the building inspector's final certificate and indeed to satisfy buyers' lawyers. The Smoke Control Association issues guidance in this matter.

Buildings over a height of 18 metres that have been externally clad with insulated cassettes require confirmation that non-combustible cladding has been used.

Ventilation commissioning certificate
Smoke and heat detectors in a new building are certified by the electrician and a certificate issued.

Solid fuel burners
Wood burners and multifuel stoves in certain areas can contribute positively to SAP ratings due to their being a sustainable energy source. They need to be registered with the Heating Equipment Testing and Approval Scheme (HETAS) upon installation. Most solid fuel burners will require the construction of a stack (chimney). It should be noted that the stack will require an internal liner and the developer should be aware that it is much easier to install the liner while the scaffold remains erected.

Flat roof guarantee
Flat roofs are often part of a roof structure either by way of an extension at single storey level or above what appears to be a pitched roof at ground level in order to reduce the height of a building. Less common perhaps is a flat roof covering the whole of the building. It is easy to overlook the requirement to have the roofing contractor supply a flat roof guarantee for labour and materials. It is, however, unlikely that the AI will overlook the requirement so it should be in place.

Security locks
External doors should have locks that comply with Part Q of the Building Regulations. It is likely that the building inspector will wish to see evidence of this prior to issuing the final certificate. The specification submitted to the supplier when seeking a quotation for the external doors should incorporate reference to Part Q Compliance.

WAT 1 Calculator (Water use)
This lists water installation types and flow rates. It is generally dealt with by the SAP specialist or M&E engineer.

Boiler guarantee
The heating boiler will have a heat loss calculation on a label on the side. This will be required for the SAP calculation upon completion.

Microgeneration Certificate Scheme
The Microgeneration Certificate Scheme (MCS) is issued by the supplier of solar panels as a guarantee of quality and workmanship of the installation. Local planning authorities are increasingly requiring renewable energy sources in new homes and photovoltaic (PV) solar panels are an efficient source of renewable energy.

Insurance
It is absolutely essential for the developer to be aware that when the final certificate is issued the Contractors All Risk (CAR) insurance no longer covers the project so the project, that is any unsold buildings, will need property insurance cover. It should also be noted that it is at this point that the AI will notify the local authority of Practical Completion (PC) and this will trigger liability for council tax.

9.3   New homes warranties
The new home warranty is often misunderstood. Many believe it was created to raise construction standards of new homes. The NHBC issues volumes of construction books that detail the requirements that the registered house-builder should apply. So construction standards are a function of the warranty. What is not always appreciated is why the new homes warranty exists in the first place. It has to do with a feature (one might almost say a 'gap') in English law. In English law there is no redress for financial loss resulting from poor workmanship for home buyers. Caveat emptor or 'let the buyer beware' applies to the purchase of property. So, no redress exists under the law of contract In the case of new homes there will no doubt be a defects liability period for snagging within the contract, say six months to sort out those minor issues that often occur.

In addition, no redress exists under the law of tort for any negligence that has caused pure economic loss (financial damage only) (see *Murphy v Brentwood DC* [1991] 1 A.C. 398). The new home buyer then potentially falls into a gap between these two potential legal remedies to any defects resulting in financial damage resulting from the purchase of property.

It should be noted that the tort of negligence would apply if physical injury occurred as a result of a builder's negligence, but we are talking here of financial loss (or pure economic loss as it is known to lawyers).

As a result of this 'gap' in the law the National House Building Council was set up in 1936 to give redress to buyers of new homes in the event of some form of construction defect by way of a warranty. This warranty is given to the buyer generally for two years for remedial works and ten years for structural work. The period generally now runs from the date of legal completion rather than that of practical completion.

The NHBC was for years the only insurer to offer this warranty but now there are many. Most offer the new homes warranty but there are those that offer a full insurance taking over the responsibility of the developer to the buyer so that the developer's liability is restricted to the period of defects liability stated in the sale contract. Such a full insurance is, of course, at additional cost to the developer but an additional benefit to the homeowner.

It is important that the developer takes out the new homes warranty when commencing the project as a condition of the warranty will be the inspection of the works as they progress. Lenders to home buyers will require evidence of a new homes warranty which will generally be a cover note prior to exchange of contracts.

New homes warranties may include deposit cover to indemnify a buyer should a developer become insolvent. This will be a commitment to see the project completed and cover for any environmental mediation that is revealed following purchase. Not all warranties, however, do include these additional indemnities.

When selecting a new homes warrantor it will save duplication to have the building inspector certify the works for the new home warrantor. The building inspector will be familiar with the project and will have approved plans and drawings.

What is clear is that compliance with the requirements of the building inspector should satisfy the new homes warrantor and visa versa which could be a case for the same surveyor undertaking both inspections.

Chapter 10

Choosing construction methods and finishes

'Simplicity is the ultimate sophistication.'
Leonardo da Vinci

I do not propose to deal with construction in this book, but merely to consider the impact that the choice of construction methods and finishes will have on the residential development project. Construction methods may impact timescales in terms of sourcing and delivery of materials and erection of buildings. Costs will be impacted by the choice of materials and the workmanship required to fit materials. Site organisation, site safety and security and storage of specialist materials may be an issue. The developer will always be aware that buyers are very sensitive to materials and finishes and could be dissuaded from buying homes that are not traditional. It is therefore essential for the developer to consider carefully the construction methods both structural and aesthetic that they will use in the project.

10.1 Masonry

This is sometimes referred to as traditional construction. The structure of the house is concrete block internal walls and a second skin of walling, either brick, stone or block, is erected externally allowing for an insulated cavity between the two walls. I prefer to use this method for high end houses particularly as I like to use underfloor heating in this type of house – with masonry construction you can use hollow concrete plank upper floors which are the better solution for underfloor central heating. Availability of masonry materials is generally good especially when ordered in advance. This traditional masonry construction is a site-based construction operation and thereby has the benefit of some flexibility should some minor design alteration be required.

10.2 Timber frame

I use panel timber frame for smaller houses and flats. Insulation levels are excellent with most timber frame and speed of construction is better than masonry but there are limitations. I do not like to use underfloor heating at first floor level within a timber floor. I am always sure to roof and tile the house prior to undertaking brickwork to allow the structure to settle under weight. I tack in some noggins for any wall units and wall hangings where I anticipate these being sited. I make an additional cost allowance for soffits and facias and some noggins and bracing of the roof structure.

It is, of course, important to appreciate that a timber frame building cannot be redesigned on site. It is fabricated in a factory and erected on site within a short period to exacting dimensions. Care needs to be taken, therefore, in the siting of ducts in the ground floor when laying the slab. The benefit is the speed of erection and the ability to get trades into the building to commence first fix.

10.3   Temporary works

It is easy to overlook temporary works. There is, of course, scaffold but there are others too that will add cost and importantly time to the project.

Scaffold will require a solid base upon which it is to be erected. The groundworker will place this but it will take time to undertake this work so this should be allowed for before ordering a timber frame delivery. Solid surfaces must also be considered for cranes close to the buildings. We try to ensure that these are positioned where drives or patios will be sited. Scaffold may also be required inside a structure to form temporary stairways, birdcage scaffold, formwork or crash decks. Signage to comply with safety requirements especially when undertaking street works off site should be considered.

When appointing a scaffolder where buildings are timber framed, the developer should ensure that this hire cost is reasonable as scaffolding will be standing for longer than with masonry construction. Scaffold inspections are a considerable additional cost. It may be possible to insist that the scaffolder carries out the scaffold inspections within their price.

If the site has a high water table, a temporary pump will be required or the project will move at a snail pace.

Road plates generally used to cover surfaces that are to be trafficked can be hired.

Equipment hire such as fork lift, accommodation, dumpers and skips are all costs which may be affected by the choices made as to the method of construction.

So, the developer must consider carefully the temporary works that will be required throughout the project and ensure that they have allowed for this in their budget.

10.4 Luxury finishes

When considering the fitting of luxury finishes to a building the developer should always be aware of the purchase cost of these materials. Luxury items are more costly to fit and often involve specialist subcontractors. They are often difficult to source too and there may be significant delays in delivery. When specifying items beyond the standard requirements it is important to bear in mind potential delays and labour.

I have just ordered an external balcony rail. It is mild steel and will be fabricated by the supplier of structural steels for the project. This supplier will fit the rail. They know the site and exactly what is required. On a previous project I ordered a glass balcony with aluminium posts. This was twice the price of mild steel. First the supplier had to survey the site and take measurements at my cost. They observed that additional work would need to be undertaken to fix the posts to existing brickwork. They came up with a design but delivery and fitting came after a great deal of correspondence. It would have been much easier to stick with the mild steel from my regular contractor.

What has to be appreciated above all is that luxury finishes often come at the end of the project. It is the point at which the bank borrowing is at its maximum and often a buyer is waiting to move in. Delays are thereby more costly than if the delay was at the beginning of the project.

10.5 Renewable energy

The principal requirement for energy efficiency is the insulation of the fabric of the building. Insulation materials are usually enclosed within a cavity wall or within the timber frame walls of the building. Roof spaces have long been subject to insulation and today no new home is constructed without insulation within the floor slab.

Renewable energy can be created by ground source heat pumps, air source heat pumps, communal (district) heating systems that run on wood chips and solid fuel, wind power and solar and PV panels. The ability of a site to create some measure of renewable energy is now a requirement in many local authority areas and will feature as a condition to the planning permission.

Ground source heat pumps

Ground source heat pumps take low grade energy from the ground through buried coils and convert it into useable energy at a higher temperature for space heating and hot water. The ground in this country is heated by the sun to an average temperature of 12°C. Collector fluid water and anti-freeze within the coils draws heat from the ground. A heat pump compresses the fluid and it is distributed throughout the house most often by underfloor heating pipework. The pressure is then reduced by expansion and the fluid is returned to the coils in the ground.

PV panels
Photovoltaic panels are the most used method of creating renewable energy in house building. These can be mounted on the surface of the roof or within the structure of the roof covering. I very much favour fitting the panels on the battening and tiling up to the panels as this gives a much neater appearance.

Air source heat pumps
The air source heat pump takes heat from the air absorbing it into a liquid refrigerant at a low temperature boosting it to a higher temperature using a compressor. It then transfers this heat to the heating system. The pump uses electricity but the energy produced is in excess of that used by the pump. Early examples of air source heat pumps in residential developments were not successful. One point to bear in mind is the need for special, larger, radiators to cope with the lower heat temperatures. This may be avoided by use of underfloor heating which will run to a lower temperature.

Energy blades
Where there is a flow of water on site from perhaps a stream or river, an energy blade can be fitted to be powered by that flow to create electricity.

I am currently having one fitted across a spillway by a millpond such that the flow is the overflow from the mill pond.

Communal heating
By this we mean heating systems designed to service more than one dwelling with space heating and hot water. They have been used in public housing schemes in this country and abroad. In Denmark I understand that 60% of housing is connected to some form of district heating system. I have used communal heating in blocks of flats to avoid independent boilers within the flats themselves. It has the benefit of requiring the servicing of just one boiler rather than many independent boilers. I see this having an advantage where flats are let with a high turnover of tenants as there is not the requirement for readings of separate systems as readings can be collectively recorded.

10.6   Climate change

We know that climate change will affect residential buildings. Buildings may be damaged by flooding, subsidence of foundations and fire in hot dry conditions.

The developer is able to incorporate in new buildings specifications that will reduce the risk of flooding and fire damage. Ground floor slabs can be raised to avoid flooding. Fire alarms have to be fitted, external materials selected to reduce fire risk and pathways for fire to travel within the building sealed.

Flood risk

Incidents of flooding have increased over recent years. For sites that are vulnerable to flooding, for example being close to streams and rivers, there may well be the requirement of a flood risk assessment undertaken by a qualified hydrologist. This will measure the ability of the site to drain satisfactorily in times of the heaviest storm and proposals for surface water drainage and floor levels made.

Foundation subsidence

Subsidence of foundations of buildings can occur when clay subsoils shrink or expand due to very dry or very wet conditions. New buildings can overcome the potential of subsidence by the adoption of piled foundations particularly when a void is incorporated under a suspended slab that will allow for movement of the subsoil known as 'heave'. A system of piles under a precast reinforced concrete slab with a 400mm void can be an excellent solution in such circumstances.

Fire risk

Extreme temperatures in America and Australia have shown us the effect of wildfires and the destruction that can result to homes. We do not generally anticipate such occurrences here in the UK but we have seen some destruction of homes resulting from wildfires here too. To date we have been shockingly made aware of the vulnerability of certain types of cladding on high rise buildings but the wholesale destruction of low-rise buildings has not been an issue. Perhaps we should do more to consider the choices we make in design and specification of new homes to ensure that fire risk is evaluated. These choices are more easily made in factory assembly of homes where greater control of materials and detailed design is available.

Chapter 11

Funding and finance

'Today, if you look at financial systems around the globe, more than half the population of the world do not qualify to take out a loan from a bank.'
Muhammad Yunus

I say again, we must consider ourselves fortunate to live in a nation with an enterprise economy that allows for the rule of law to govern our ability to borrow funds for development of property; property that provides security to the lender through identification, registration and valuation; availability of services that are guaranteed at a reasonable price to all citizens; infrastructure by way of highways and railways, schools and colleges, shops and offices and places of work that allow demand for our developments. Without security, loans would not be available. Without infrastructure, residential development projects may be left unsold and unwanted.

It is against this background that development takes place and that the opportunities exist for the deployment of capital.

Residential development projects are expensive to acquire and to undertake. The developer will generally need to arrange finance for the project. That finance will necessarily be available throughout the project as it progresses. This funding will be either from a clearing bank, specialist property lending bank, peer-to-peer lender or private finance through joint venture or investors. Whatever the source, finance is one of the critical factors of property development along with location and timing.

What has to be appreciated is that whatever the source and method of funding the developer's profit will likely be realised only on the final sale of a small project and until that final sale is completed, the developer will have to provide their own working capital. It is essential that they make provision for working capital either from their own resources or by securing a project management fee within the construction loan from the funder.

I have experienced a variety of methods of funding development projects and I can confirm that there are advantages and disadvantages to all of them.

11.1   Funders

Funding for development projects can come from a whole range of sources. There are clearing banks such as NatWest, Lloyds and Barclays and specialist banks that lend only for residential development. Crowdfunding has become quite prominent as well as peer-to-peer lending which provides an online platform for collaborative investment in property development that many see as a key player in future projects. Then there are of course wealthy individuals who see the advantage of a higher rate of interest than they would earn from other investments or who are prepared to join in the risk of the project by way of joint venture.

11.2   Clearing banks

In the past, clearing banks were the first to be approached by developers. The big four dominated the residential property lending market and loans were relatively easy to obtain, particularly for those borrowers with a good track record as established developers.

The bank's loan is secured by way of first legal charge on the project itself and is thus termed senior debt. Terms usually include an interest rate of between 7% and 10% per annum plus an arrangement fee of 1% to 1.5 % of the money borrowed. The total facility will be between 60% and 65% of the projected GDV as endorsed by the bank's valuer. The borrower is therefore required to make a contribution and this is usually input upon the acquisition of the project rather than at a later stage in the programme. If the site is being acquired at a favourable price less than the market valuation, then the borrower's contribution might be lower than if a full market price is being paid.

Example

Purchase price of site	£1,500,000
Building costs/fees	£1,500,000
GDV	£4,000,000
Loan at 65% GDV	£2,600,000

The developer's contribution here would be £400,000. That is the loan of £2,600,000 less the building costs and fees of £1,500,000 which leaves a sum of £ 1,100,000 to meet the purchase price of £1,500,000. The £400,000 would be required upon the acquisition of the site so that the developer would draw down £1,100,000 from the bank upon completion of the purchase and make up the balance of £400,000 from their own resources. The bank would retain the £1,500,000 building costs and fees for incremental advance as the project progresses.

Additional terms might be that an amount to cover bank interest is to be set aside by the lender. The initial loan may then be reduced to allow for projected interest. Here it might be £200,000 making the developer's contribution upon first drawdown £600,000. The terms may include a charge to be taken over shares in the borrowing company and that personal guarantees should be given by the directors of the company. Less commonly, collateral security might be given by way of a charge on property that is not directly associated with the project.

Established developers may be able to obtain roll over finance terms where funds are not designated to any particular project but 'roll over' to the next one. This is advantageous, as the developer can plan their acquisitions in the knowledge that finance has been arranged. Such facilities are unlikely to be available to an inexperienced developer.

While such clearing bank funding can be at reasonable interest rates, perhaps 7%, with lending terms at say 60% LTV, it is clearly not always sufficient to provide adequate funds for the project and the developer may therefore be obliged to seek a source of junior debt – a further loan, often referred to as mezzanine funding (see below).

11.3   Specialist property lending banks
There are a number of specialist banks who provide finance as senior lenders but at a blended rate that incorporates the senior debt rate and part of the mezzanine requirement at a higher rate.

Typically, such a specialist lender will provide lending to 70% of GDV, an additional 10% over the clearing bank level. They therefore 'blend' the senior debt interest on the 60% with the junior debt interest rate on the balance resulting in a higher rate.

The advantage of using a specialist lender is often the expertise they are able to demonstrate and the speed with which they are able to respond. Specialist banks are less likely to question contractual provisions between the developer and the contractor within a JCT contract. They may be less insistent on amendments and on funders' collateral warranties from the entire design team. This may be beneficial to the developer who wishes to use a standard JCT design build contract with a standard collateral warranty signed by the contractor.

11.4 Mezzanine funders

The mezzanine loan is the additional funds borrowed over and above the lending bank's facility. The mezzanine loan will be secured on the project by way of second charge behind the first charge to the lending bank. It is therefore at greater risk than the bank's facility and the interest rate paid for the mezzanine loan will reflect that greater risk. Where a lending bank might be at 8%, a mezzanine loan could be at 20%. Typically, the mezzanine lender will not 'top up' the funding to the full extent of costs expecting the developer to have made some contribution. It is beneficial that the developer is able to pay off the mezzanine finance ahead of the senior debt if the bank is happy to allow this. For example, where houses are complete the lending bank may be prepared to have the site revalued and to increase the senior debt making the mezzanine debt at its higher interest rate available for repayment.

11.5 Crowdfunding

A crowdfund is an internet-based platform where investors with small amounts of money can collaborate to provide equity to a project requiring a greater amount than any one of them may be able to invest. The project can be any type of business but there is always an interest in property funding given the inherent security of property and the relatively short period of the project. There are therefore crowdfunders who specialise in providing equity for small residential development projects subject to a share of the profit.

The benefit for investors is the ability to invest a small amount of money in a specific project and the generally high rate of return that is offered. The crowdfunder will undertake the due diligence and make available online all information such that the investor does not have to undertake their own investigation. The funds will be deposited for a pre-arranged period calculated to allow completion of the sales of the development. This might typically be for two years. Security is provided by a charge on the project and a simple contract is entered into with the crowdfunders' trustee company for loan notes.

Often the offer will be for shares in a special purpose company that is set up for a single development giving the investors a share of the profit made from the development.

11.6 Peer-to-peer lending

Peer-to-peer lending for residential development operates via an online platform that advertises a development project for collaborative investment where a large number of investors can contribute.

It is usually a loan to the developer at a fixed interest rate. Generally I have found peer-to-peer lenders to be keen to lend senior debt and not mezzanine loans. Therefore, a first charge on the site will be in place for the investor's security. Investors are invited to invest in specific projects selected by the peer-to-peer lender and subject to due diligence by the peer-to-peer lender. Projects are usually well subscribed particularly in areas of high demand. Investors have to recognise that while returns may be higher than investments in a bank there is of course the risk that if a project does not sell, the invested capital may be at risk. For the developer, however, the funding arrangement is very similar to that of the specialist bank. The difference is more the manner in which the funding is raised.

11.7 Private funders and Joint Venture funding

A private investor is simply someone who invests in a project. Often these funds are junior debt secured behind the senior debt and generally therefore at a higher rate of interest to reflect the greater risk. The investor will have a second charge on the site and that of course means that they will be vulnerable to any decline in the market and subject to the directions of the first chargee if the security is taken into possession. They will receive repayment following repayment of the senior debt.

Often private investors prefer to take a profit rather than interest and therefore they become joint venture (JV) partners. A joint venture partner might put up 100% of funds in a project in return for 50% of the profit possibly incorporating a reduced rate of interest on the invested funds as a preferred profit. The deal will depend on the anticipated profit and how keen the investor is to invest. The developer will be responsible for the acquisition and planning of the project at their own risk and supervise the project management and possibly the construction and sale of the project.

The JV partner funding the development to 100% can quite reasonably expect to take ownership of the site subject to a joint venture agreement with the developer. The JV agreement should be absolutely clear as to responsibilities of the parties. Matters that appear small at the outset may become enlarged. What happens if the project takes much longer than expected to sell? Is the construction contract sum to be fixed? If it is, does it include fees which will always be variable. Who is to fund maintenance and service costs while completed property is standing? In my experience it is often the developer who undertakes this and funds these costs. Are they to receive interest on financial inputs they make? JV agreements should ensure that they do.

Joint ventures with landowners

An obvious party to approach to act as a joint venture partner is the site owner. The developer will not, however, be able to borrow construction funds from a lender where the site owner is a joint venture partner unless the site owner is prepared to allow the site to be placed as security for the loan. It may be that with a deal structured in this way the site owner secures the finance with the developer acting as a contractor and thereby not responsible for raising the development finance. In such circumstances the developer will no doubt be required to provide some sort of guarantee as to costs.

Enabling development

There are developers who specialise in development which involves the landowner as joint venture partner. Often this is what is termed 'enabling development' as it enables a facility to be constructed for the landowner in return for land that can be developed for housing. Examples of this are where a church or youth hostel requires their accommodation to be reconstructed and a deal is set up with a developer who is to construct the facility along with a block of flats over or by the facility. For the developer such an arrangement can be beneficial as there is no requirement, or a lesser requirement, for the land to be purchased at the outset of the development of the project as the purchase price is effectively the building of the facility for the site owner. Again, the developer has to recognise that they are unlikely under such arrangements to be able to offer security to their funder in respect of the construction finance as the site will remain in the ownership of the JV partner.

Percentage of selling price of the development

Another joint venture arrangement that can save the expenditure on land at the outset of a project is where the land is paid for as a percentage of the selling price of the site as developed when sold. Clearly this arrangement is dependent on a vendor willing to await the proceeds of his sale of the land until the project is complete. Usually, the percentage paid from sale proceeds will exceed the residual land figure as it will incorporate an amount reflecting interest saved on a land purchase. It should, however, again be noted that funders of such schemes may be hesitant to lend where there is no first charge available on the land and such a deal may require the landowner to grant such a charge to the developer's funding bank for the construction finance. For this reason, a percentage of selling price deals are generally struck by national developers acquiring large sites from large corporations or public bodies.

Mini bonds

Some developers raise funds through an offer of what have been termed mini bonds. These are unregulated investments and very risky for the investor. Recently we have witnessed several scams where funds are raised and not put into projects but spent in fees to companies related to the fund raisers. London Capital Finance and Blackmore bonds are reported as having done this. However, where the funds raised are genuinely placed into property, whether a development or standing property, if there is a legal charge to the fund raising entity there is no reason why a mini bond cannot be a reasonable method of fund raising.

Promotion agreements

It is not only a contractor developer who can engage in a joint venture with a landowner. Many developers who are land use and project planning specialists also enter into such agreements. Here the developer's role is to secure a planning permission that enhances land value and undertake the project planning that creates the 'oven ready' site for sale to a housebuilder. The sale price is then split in some way between the developer and the landowner. Agreements of this kind are sometimes referred to as 'promotion agreements'. The advantage to the developer in such agreements is that there is a more limited requirement for borrowing from a bank as they are not undertaking the project themselves and their exit from the deal will be sooner. The developer will, however, be at risk for the costs of formulation and submission of the planning application.

11.8   Mortgage brokers

A mortgage broker acts for the borrower in securing finance for the development project. They may charge a fee to the borrower for this though often they are remunerated by the lender. They are obliged if they receive payment from the lender to advise the borrower of this.

A good broker will have many contacts in the funding market and will be aware of current availability of funds and terms. They will deal with a wide range of funders and are often very professional with a wide understanding of their requirements. Many brokers are authorised and regulated by the Financial Conduct Authority.

11.9   Costs of finance

When looking at the cost of finance one inevitably looks at the interest rate to be charged. This is, of course, relevant but there are additional costs to consider.

The bank will charge an arrangement fee which may be at 1.5% of the loan and possibly an exit fee of a similar amount. An exit fee calculated on the GDV rather than the loan is sometimes charged, and in my view should be resisted. It should be charged on the amount of the loan facility not GDV. The bank will expect the borrower to pay its lawyer's costs and these will be charged upon acceptance of the facility and instruction of the bank's lawyer. Many specialist banks will employ a monitoring surveyor to approve the costs submitted by the borrower and to carry out inspections on a monthly basis throughout the project. Again, this will be at the cost of the developer. The valuation of the site will be prepared by another specialist surveyor listed on the bank's panel. Again, this fee will be paid by the borrower. So additional costs of obtaining finance are: arrangement fee, exit fee, valuation fee, project monitor's fee, bank's solicitor's fee and broker's fee if applicable.

11.10   The terms of a loan

A lending bank will issue a loan facility letter setting out the particulars of the loan together with the terms. Typically, it will state the whole loan facility, the name of the borrowing entity, and the amount and purpose of the loan. The loan facility will then be divided into separate amounts: the site advance is the amount the bank is to contribute to the acquisition of the project; the development advance is the amount the bank will contribute to the construction cost; the professional fees advance is the amount for fees; and there will be a retention from the loan facility of amounts for interest, set aside to pay the bank, and arrangement fee.

Generally, the lending bank will require 100% of sale proceeds as houses are sold.

The lending bank will require security and guarantees which will usually be a debenture over the borrower's assets. The borrower will be an SPC and thereby this debenture will be over the assets of the SPC and its share capital. Personal guarantees from the shareholders or directors of the borrower and cost overrun guarantees to a fixed level may also be required.

Conditions precedent to the loan facility being drawn down will need to be satisfied prior to the acquisition. Usually, the terms will also include conditions subsequent to the first drawdown, these conditions to be satisfied following acquisition of the site. They will include evidence of the building contract and collateral warranties and insurances.

11.11 Viabilities

Today, no serious developer would not calculate a cashflow of the project that incorporates all costs to establish land value and profit. There are two ways of assessing this. First the residual valuation. This is a valuation that deducts all costs from the GDV to leave a sum for the land referred to as the residual value. A simple example of this appears at Chapter 6. Then there is the cashflow viability. This is a more detailed approach to the valuation of the project which includes an accumulation of all costs associated with the development project over a project programme to assess the profit. The experienced developer will maintain a record of build cost per square metre of gross area and apply this to a viability. To this they will add extra over costs for such things as off site sewers, estate road, fees and other costs.

11.12 Funding the acquisition of the site

The acquisition of the site usually takes place with an exchange of the contract to purchase with legal completion up to four weeks later. Where several tranches of land or other legal interests are being acquired together, it is usual to arrange the acquisition of all of these simultaneously. To fail to do so may leave the developer with a part of the site with an intending vendor in a position to increase their sale price.

The bank will have set out its offer of funding and the developer should review this prior to exchange of the contract to ensure that they have calculated the numbers correctly and are not left with a shortfall of funds on legal completion.

They should note that the bank will retain from its offer a sum for its interest, fees and any CIL or section 106 sums due to the planning authority. The developer should be clear as to the amount of funds that the bank is going to transfer on completion.

11.13 Costs and fees on purchase

The developer must be aware of the costs and fees to be paid upon purchase of the project to avoid the embarrassment of insufficient funds on completion. These will include:

* Stamp Duty Land Tax (SDLT);

- the bank's arrangement fee (which is generally deducted from the first drawdown at usually 1.5%);

- the bank's lawyer's fee and its surveyor's fees (both valuation and site monitoring). The developer may well be required to pay these up front prior to professionals being instructed;

- valuation fee; and

- any indemnity insurance premiums required to ensure that the security is robust.

Rates of SDLT have risen substantially in recent years. All buyers need to submit a form to HMRC via the lawyer on completion stating the amount of SDLT the buyer will be paying. One particularly onerous rate is the 3% addition for companies acquiring residential sites. The additional SDLT applies even when a residential building is being demolished to make way for new homes.

Commercial rates of SDLT apply where any part of a site being acquired is commercial and the rate is generally more favourable than the rates for residential sites. If any small part of the site is commercial, the commercial rate applies. Note that the commercial rate also applies where six residential plots or more are being acquired. SDLT rates can be calculated online via the SDLT rate calculator. Where a building to be demolished has been used as a residence, its gross internal area is deducted from the computation of the gross internal area of the proposal.

11.14   Charges

The lender will take a charge as security for the loan. Senior debt will always be secured by way of a legal charge on the title of the property and thus registered at the Land Registry. A charge can also be taken as an equitable charge, sometimes referred to as a 'soft charge', which does not allow the holder the power of sale of the property. The holder of a legal charge has to give consent for a second legal charge but not for an equitable charge.

11.15   Project accounts

If a developer is undertaking a number of projects at one time, it will be essential to ensure that costs are allocated to the correct project. I have separate ring-fenced accounts for each project including those that are not yet ready to commence construction work, thus are incurring only pre-construction fees. This prevents invoices for project A getting mixed up with those for project B and this is particularly important where a joint venture partner is involved in A but not B. I have a general company account as well to ensure that those costs that cannot be allocated to a project – company accounts, wages, and rent for example – are kept separate from the projects.

Some specialist banks will prefer to pay suppliers direct rather than the developer. Where amounts are paid to a supplier the developer must be sure not to overlook them in calculating the total loan received from the lender.

11.16   Project Monitoring Surveyor initial report and monthly application for drawdown of funds.

At the end of each month funds will be drawn down from the lender to pay for labour and materials engaged by and fitted to the buildings in the project. A development loan will have been arranged with the funder. The funder will have allocated a maximum facility, generally up to 65% of GDV. The construction costs submitted by the developer and agreed by the lender's Project Monitoring Surveyor (PMS) will be drawn down from an amount retained by the lender to meet costs during the course of the project. The balance of the bank's loan after the construction loan will be drawn down to assist with the site acquisition.

The funder will employ its PMS, who will be a chartered surveyor engaged by the bank, to analyse the project documents and the monthly application for funds to ensure that the project remains on budget and on programme.

It is, of course, as well for a developer to be prepared in the provision of this information to the PMS to speed up the process. They should agree that a certain amount of this information can be provided following first drawdown of the facility but before construction begins. Let us consider what the PMS will need to review to enable their initial report to the funder.

(1)   Viability.

This is a spreadsheet showing data inputs, cashflow and residual valuation. A copy of the valuation report showing comparable sale prices and estimated sales values will support this viability.

(2)   Contract sum analysis.

This is a breakdown of the total building cost showing the amount ascribed to each trade. The PMS will need to see that the amount allocated is sufficient for the project.

(3) Letters of Appointment of professionals in the design team setting out the terms of the appointment.

These will include: architect, structural and civil engineers, principal designer and any other professionals whose design or report may need to be relied upon.

(4) Building contract.

This is the signed contract between the developer and main contractor. This is required even if the developer and the contractor are the same team. They will be separate companies and therefore there is requirement for a building contract. Incidentally, the contract may be useful to the developer if they are ever challenged by HMRC as to zero-rating VAT supplies.

(5) Collateral warranties to the funder.

The collateral warranty to the funder (CWa/F) creates a legally binding relationship between the warrantor and the lender. It is used where design is input into a scheme. The parties who may therefore be required to give such a warranty are those involved in some aspect of the design.

Contractor
The loan will be to the developer so the contractor is not within the privity of contract applying to the facility. They will therefore need to sign a collateral warranty.

Architect
The architect will inevitably have a large input to the design and specification.

Structural engineer
The structural engineer will have produced, or will produce, plans showing foundations and structural elements.

Civil engineer
They will have designed drainage layouts and road works.

Piling contractor
(This might also cover the developer where the piling contractor is engaged by a groundwork subcontractor). This warranty will usually be submitted to the PMS prior to construction rather than prior to acquisition of the project.

Timber frame or floor beam company
If timber frame is being used, this will be a substantial design input. With masonry construction, first floor beams are usually hollow concrete supplied and fitted by specialist suppliers. They will require some form of guarantee or warranty.

Collateral warranties are notoriously difficult to secure from certain members of the professional team. The developer should always state, when inviting tender for engagement of design professionals, that they will be required to sign a collateral warranty for a funder.

(6)   Health and safety statements.

The principal contractor's plan is prepared by the contractor to identify risks in the project and how these might be addressed.

The site management plan is the plan that sets out the location of those matters essential to the construction process, for example cabins, storage, parking, WCs and skips.

(7)   Drawings.

Planning drawings: Floor plans. Elevations. Sections. Site layout.

Working drawings: Piling plan. Services. Drainage. Landscape plan.

(8)   Copies of planning permissions.

Principal consent.

Approval of conditions.

(9)   Assumption of Liability Notices submitted to LPA relating to CIL.

(10) Section 106 planning agreement where this has been required.

(11) Insurances.

Professional indemnity insurances of the design team.

(12) New home warranty.

Offer from new home warranty provider. The actual warranty is issued to the eventual buyer following legal completion but some evidence that this is in place is generally sufficient.

(13) Confirmation of Approved Inspector.

I ask the new homes warrantor to appoint the AI. In this way the AI can report for both the statutory inspection and the warranty.

(14) Confirmation of drainage authority permission to connect to public sewer (section 106 Water Industry Act 1991).

(15) Street name confirmation from local authority together with numbering of dwellings.

(16) Fees schedule.

Fees spent to date and to be spent. These may constitute an additional separate loan facility from the bank.

(17) Reports from consultants.

Trees. Ecology. Hydrology. Heritage. Environmental. Soils. Acoustic.

Monthly application
An application to draw down finance will be made to the bank via the PMS who will visit the site to agree a valuation of the works undertaken and assess any claim for pre-payments.

It is important that the monthly application to the PMS is accurate as to the claim and supported by invoices or documents received from subcontractors and suppliers if required.

The application might be based on the Contract Sum Analysis (CSA) produced at the time the loan was being agreed. It will therefore be a spreadsheet showing monthly and cumulated expenditure for each trade against the budget thereby revealing the saving or overspend in cost. This will allow the PMS to see more clearly the cost trends of the project and to advise the bank accordingly. The developer has to understand that any overspend is unlikely to be met by the bank as the build cost in the CSA reflects the bank's commitment, unless a contingency has been allowed in the figures.

The bank's PMS will also require updates of professional consultants' insurances when renewed, copies of building inspector's reports and health and safety reports as they are issued.

If the developer has budgeted a project management fee, this should be included in each monthly application divided equally between the months of the project. In this way a cashflow can be created throughout the project to pay site wages and general expenses. I invoice my construction company monthly from a project management partnership so I become just another professional working on the project.

Dealing with finance for a development project can be very time consuming and requires detailed analysis of figures. There is always the danger of costs over-running budgets and as funders have become far more cautious over the years I have worked in the industry, any cost over-runs will likely be required to be met by the developer.

I would always recommend a developer spreads risk by taking on joint venture projects, construction contracts of some kind, or perhaps site sales to balance finances where they are involved in a more speculative development project.

That having been said, development can reap substantial profits when managed well by a developer who has the vision to create a project for which there is demand and the knowledge and understanding of the requirements.

Case study 8
Finance
Key issue: Obtaining finance for a project in property.

When you are confronted by a deal that seems too good to turn down it is frustrating if funds are already employed elsewhere or for other reasons unavailable. The deal may have come as a result of another party failing to go ahead perhaps for the very reason that they too do not have funds available. In this case, the deal came to my company as we had dealt successfully with an adjoining project and it seemed logical for the vendor to approach us first. The issue was therefore the funding of the project.

First, you should consider the alternative funding methods, for example bank funds from a specialist property lender who generally lends up to 70% of GDV – certainly no more and often less. This then requires the developer to come up with a contribution and if they are working on a 15% profit margin, their contribution will be 15%.

This contribution is worked out as follows:

If a 15% profit margin is required, costs will be 100% (GDV) – 15% = 85%

The bank will lend 70% of GDV.

This leaves the developer having to make up 100% – 15% – 70% = 15%.

This can be a significant amount to raise and it should be pointed out that there are factors that can distort this equation such as:

- the possibility of a down valuation reducing the GDV and thereby the loan available;

- the costs of acquisition that need to be met by the developer;

- the bank loan being reduced by the retention of interest such that a lesser percentage is available.

This means the expectation of a deal with no developer contribution is questionable.

Secondly, I would advise seeing how the project sits within the current projects being undertaken. Is the developer carrying out exclusively speculative projects with bank funding or is there a spread of activity across speculative development, custom-build client and housing association project management and perhaps joint venture development? A developer who gambles on every development they take on and being speculative with high levels of bank funding is running the risk that they will run out of cash.

This deal as I have said was attractive and not one that we would wish to hand over to a private client.

In this case the solution was not difficult to establish. A joint venture partner willing to put in the whole funding for 50% of the profit was the answer. In this way, funds were assured and existing projects could progress unaffected by the subject deal. The attractiveness of the deal meant that a joint venture partner was easy to attract and there would be enough profit for each party.

Chapter 12

Legal requirements of a development project

'Freedom and Property Rights are inseparable. You can't have one without the other.'
George Washington

This book is not a law book. The further reading schedule refers the reader to several excellent law books which will be useful for additional reading on many of the subjects in this book. I have, however, made several very necessary references to legal statutes and cases throughout the text to illustrate sources of law.

Let us first remind ourselves why the rule of law is such an important ingredient in property. Why is it inseparable from freedom? Hernando de Soto, in his book *The Mystery of Capital*, exposes the disfunction of economies without the rule of law. Law gives us legislation that ensures that the weak are not exploited by the strong and the poor are not exploited by the rich. It gives us the ability to resolve disputes through authorised independent jurisdiction or adjudication. It allows us to limit liability through limited companies and partnerships. It safeguards the public realm with planning control and building regulation. It provides for the availability of services to buildings available to all. It gives us procedures for the transfer of private property rights and it gives us the mechanism for the registration of title such that we can be sure of the ownership and extent of property.

It is then the rule of law that provides the framework for the enterprise economy. We have legislation that sets out a fair and level playing field. Those who are wronged have the right to seek redress. We have an economy within which risk is measurable and reward given. Property provides the dignity of ownership and security for finance.

The study of property law covers such subjects as land law, construction law, planning law, environmental law, landlord and tenant law and contract and tort law. Property law is therefore very much part of the development process in that it influences so many of the decisions that need to be made in residential development projects. Certainly, there is no substitute for a good lawyer to handle transactions and advise generally, but a basic knowledge of aspects of property law will be of great value in an understanding of how residential development projects work.

I have divided this chapter into Part 1 and Part 2. Part 1 explains the legal issues that will almost certainly be confronted in acquiring and undertaking a residential development project and in Part 2 I have attempted to describe some additional matters that might be encountered and those which may expand knowledge in the subject.

Part 1

12.1 Contracts and options

For an agreement to purchase land to be enforceable there will need to be a legally binding contract or option to purchase. This will need to be in writing. The developer should not assume that there will be any moral or legal obligation on the vendor to allow them to proceed with the purchase of a site with a mere gentleman's agreement once substantial value has been added by obtaining planning permission. An agreement for the sale and purchase of land has to be in writing and signed by both parties. The case of *Yeoman's Row Management Ltd & Anor v Cobbe* [2008] UKHL 55 illustrates the wisdom of getting a firm legal agreement in writing drawn up by a solicitor prior to a developer adding a very substantial value to an intending vendor's land.

Contracts

A contract to purchase a property must be legally enforceable. It has to have the following ingredients of a contract; it has to identify the property, the parties selling and buying it, it has to be intended to create a legal relationship to be signed by both parties and there has to be some kind of consideration.

The property

The address is often given a brief description, then the title number and often, a plan showing the property boundaries outlined in red.

The parties

The parties to a contract are those who can enforce it through the rule known as privity of contract. While there is nowadays the opportunity to allow third parties to enforce the benefit of a contract this is rare in practice (Contracts (Rights of Third Parties) Act 1999). The buyer should consider at the point of exchange of the contract whether they are happy with the entity they are to employ to enter into the contract. There may be a reason to alter the contracting party, for example if it has been agreed to enter into some form of joint venture arrangement. I always like to expressly ensure that I can assign the benefit of the contract by a clause stating this.

Signing the contract

A contract can be a deed but it rarely is. It therefore does not need to be witnessed but, while a deed is said to 'impute' consideration, a contract requires consideration.

Consideration

The contract must have some form of consideration. The legal term of consideration is that given for the contract, often a promise or an amount of money. It is perhaps more accurate to say, 'A valuable consideration in the sense of the law may consist either in some right, interest, profit, or benefit accruing to one party, or some forbearance, detriment, loss or responsibility given, suffered or undertaken by another' (see *Currie v Misa* (1875) LR 10 Ex 153).

Notwithstanding the breadth of this definition, an amount of money is most often the most convenient consideration given for an option. It does not need to be a significant amount of money. £1 will be sufficient.

Options

An option can be described as a unilateral contract. Again, it requires the ingredients of a contract but the party to whom the option is granted is the only one who may enforce the deal. They are not giving a promise as they have the option not to go ahead. They therefore have to give consideration – generally the consideration will be money and legally £1 is valuable consideration. It may be necessary to make such an arrangement attractive to the other party. I once came across an option granted by an intending vendor to a developer for a consideration of £5,000 per month. The option was open to be rescinded if the intending buyer failed to pay the consideration. The agreement was designed to give the developer the opportunity to obtain planning permission but alas that permission was never granted. The consideration is often recoverable by deduction to the purchase price so here, with no deal eventuating, it was lost to the vendor by the intending buyer.

Generally, the developer has a commitment to formulate and submit plans at their own cost and given the cost of the plans and reports required, I consider that sufficient to be, in practice, the consideration for the option.

Assigning an option
To be absolutely transparent, I always like to make it clear that the option is assignable as, over the period of negotiating a planning permission, the developer may well have changed their plans as to which entity they wish to undertake the development in, or indeed they may wish to assign the option to a third party having obtained planning consent.

Waiver clause
I always like to ensure that I am able to waive the requirement that planning permission is granted. If planning permission is refused, I may well wish to proceed with the purchase aware that I will be granted planning permission eventually and that I am buying at a good price. For the avoidance of doubt, the ability to acquire the site if planning permission is refused should be clear.

12.2   Heads of terms
Heads of terms (HoT) are not a legal requirement but a useful way of setting out the agreement between buyer and seller at the outset, noting any matters that are likely to create issues and indicating timescales. It is usual to agree heads of terms with the vendor to avoid any misunderstandings such that this can be sent to solicitors with instructions giving them a broad outline of the deal and the wishes of the parties. The HoT is not, however, a document that can be relied upon after exchange of a contract. The contract is assumed to include all the details of the deal and the HoT will thereby be superseded by the contract following its exchange.

12.3   Title
Much of the land in Britain is registered at the Land Registry. The registry records the titles of property, their ownership and what benefits and restrictions apply to them.

It is useful to bear in mind the words of Windyer J in *Breskar v Wall* [1971] 126 C.L.R. 376 that registration is 'a source of title rather than a retrospective approbation of it as a derivative right'. This is reflected in section 69 Land Registration Act 2002 which provides a 'statutory magic' vesting the title in the proprietor regardless of any irregularity in the transfer itself.

This means simply that, when you read the title of a piece of land, you do not need to look behind it and question whether it really is owned by the proprietor shown on the register. The Land Registry guarantees that it does. So, the registered land is a source of title not merely a reflection of what the landowner has cobbled together for the registry to record. The buyer may rely on it.

When buying a car, you would want to see the log book to establish who owns it. It is the same with property. The title will be in the name of the owner or owners and, in most cases, they will be the people the buyer is dealing with. But the title to property will tell the buyer more about the property than a log book will about a car so it is definitely worth them spending some time examining the title.

Under English law we have a system of registration of land titles. This means that upon transfer, the title is registered at the Land Registry in the buyer's name and any fresh rights, responsibilities and dispositions of part of the title recorded. The registration comprises three registers: the property register which shows the address of the property and any legal rights it benefits by; the proprietorship register stating who owns it; and the charges register stating the third party rights the property is subject to. There is also a plan showing the curtilage of the property outlined in red. This sounds very straightforward and indeed in many cases it is. Occasionally, however, the buyer sees the title to the property they are buying with a multitude of covenants and a plan drawn up in all the colours of a fruit salad.

The most important fact to consider about the registers is that the Land Registry is providing a guarantee of the accuracy of the information. Indeed Chief Justice Barwick has said, '*Ours is not a system of registration of title, but a system of title by registration.*'

We should not, therefore, be surprised that there are strict rules relating to registration of title. We cannot simply invent our own version of legal rights and seek their registration. While it is often commented that land law does not change on any regular basis, we must recognise the possibility that servitudes and easements 'might expand with the changes that take place in the circumstances of mankind' (per Lord St Leonard in *Dyce v Lady Jane Hay* (1852) 1 Macq 305).

Property register
The property register can be said to record the advantageous aspects of the property. It contains a description of the land and notes matters such as easements, rights and privileges which inure for the benefit of the land. It may not, however, record the benefit of restrictive covenants over adjoining property.

Proprietorship register

This gives the name and address of the proprietor whether the title is described as absolute or good leasehold, qualified or possessory together with any restrictions on disposition of the interest.

Charges register

The minor interests are recorded here (see Land Charges Act 1972). These will be restrictions, cautions, inhibitions and notices, covenants, easements and finance charges. In short anything to which the property is 'negatively' affected. So these notices, easements and restrictive covenants in the charges register will be those to which the property is subject, not those that benefit the property.

Inspection of the register

The implementation of the Land Registry Act 1988 saw a significant change in the mystery that surrounded the ownership of land. Members of the public upon payment of a fee can now inspect the register to see who owns land although they are not able to see details of financial charges. The register is available online which is a considerable advantage over the situation when I started in the business. This does not apply to unregistered land as that does not, of course, appear in the register.

Overriding interests

Just when you think you might be understanding this subject, I want to mention something that can potentially have you wondering how solid this guarantee of title is. I refer to overriding interests.

These were introduced by section 70 Land Registration Act 1925 and are now set out in Schedule 3 Land Registration Act 2002.

There are a number of interests that bind a transferee of registered land notwithstanding that they are not recorded on the register. That is to say, the transferee purchases a site but certain rights still override their interest in the site even though they are not recorded in the title document.

The most significant of these is the rights of persons in actual occupation. In practice pre-contract enquiries will expose such occupation so this is not generally an issue for a developer buyer. One may wish to note that unrecorded legal easements are an overriding interest.

12.4   The transfer

The transfer is the deed signed by both parties to enable completion of the purchase. It will contain covenants by both transferor and transferee. The transfer might exclude potential claims arising such as that easements shall be by express grant only. It might clarify that the fresh covenants do not constitute a building scheme.

The developer will be concerned to review the transfer of the land parcels making up the site they are to purchase and to be aware of any limitations that might threaten their proposals. They will also need to be sure that there are no restrictions that will inhibit the funding of the site.

The transfer will describe the tenure of the property, whether freehold or leasehold. If leasehold there will be a lease to sign upon exchange of contracts.

The transfer will show any third party rights over the property and describe rights reserved and granted. Where the development is to comprise a number of properties the developer will need to consider carefully what fresh rights require to be granted to each of the buyers of the properties they are to sell. For example, all will require access and services but there may be cross easements to connect say Plot 2 across Plot 1. Care must be taken not to transfer communal facilities to any one of the properties. I once saw a bicycle shed transferred to the ground floor flat. It must have been difficult for the developer to unravel this error and potentially could prevent subsequent sales of the remaining flats.

Restrictions will be shown together with the identity of parties in benefit of those restrictions.

So the developer may purchase their site with a brief understanding of the contract, title and transfer untroubled by any requirement to delve further into the subject of property law. However, given my impression that a wider understanding of property law is often required, I list below in Part 2 some further information.

Part 2

This is a summary of some legal terms that are encountered in the development of projects in property.

12.5   Easements

An easement is a proprietary right over the land of another for the benefit of other land which generally adjoins the land subject to the easement. It does not give an exclusive right and, as a proprietary right, it runs with the land and is not personal to the owner.

Examples of easements are rights of way and drainage rights across neighbouring land. In the case of *Re Ellenborough Park* (1956) Ch 131, the Master of the Rolls had to consider four tenets that apply to an easement. First there have to be two areas of land. These are called the dominant and the servient tenement. Second, these tenements have to be separately owned. Third, the easement has to benefit the dominant tenement and finally it has to be capable of being the subject matter of a grant.

Easements can be implied in a transfer of land. For example, a developer purchases B, part of an area of land known as ABC owned by Smith to which access is gained over the land to be retained by Smith AC. The access was not supported by an existing legal easement because all of ABC was owned by Smith and for an easement to exist, the two areas of land have to be separately owned. This easement is implied and is known as the rule in *Wheeldon v Burrows* (1879) 12 Ch D 31. Section 62 Law of Property Act 1925 essentially converts informal rights into legal rights and thereby, upon transfer of the legal estate, informal easements may become legal easements (see *Hair v Gilman* (2000) 80 P. & C.R. 108).

The important point about implied easements is that the vendor's lawyer will often ensure that the transfer will exclude section 62 and *Wheeldon v Burrows*, and therefore the buyer will not be able to rely on them. It is essential then that the lawyer is alert to any fresh easements that require to be granted for the benefit of the completed project.

When you buy a tranche of land you are buying not only the buildings on it but the easements that go with it. This is because you are actually buying the property, the rights and responsibilities appurtenant to the land and the buildings on it. Section 62 Law and Property Act 1925 says that the purchase of land shall be deemed to include easements rights and advantages appertaining to the land, land being defined as the land and buildings thereon.

So, an easement is a third party right over land owned by someone other than the party benefitting from the easement. That is to say, the grantee cannot have an easement over his own land, it has to be someone else's land. For this reason when buying part of a land holding, the developer will need to consider what fresh easements may need to be created so that each part of the land sub-divided has in place the easements necessary for it to operate the requirements of the project when complete.

It is advisable when creating an easement by grant to require it to be for all purposes. The grant of an easement of access may not be sufficient if the intention is to run services and drainage under that access. The deed should be clear as to what is required and the route that the easement will cross over the servient land clarified.

12.6   Freehold restrictive covenants

A freehold restrictive covenant can be so restrictive as to potentially prevent development altogether. Where a restrictive covenant appears on the title it is something to be considered carefully as an early part of the due diligence. The covenant has to benefit land close by and is usually the result of part of a land holding having been sold off, with the balance land granted the benefit of a covenant as to how the land sold may be used. That covenant will, if restrictive not positive, run with the land in benefit and can therefore be enforced by subsequent owners of the land in benefit.

If the title of a site is subject to a covenant restricting development in some way there are two factors to potentially advantage the developer owning the land subject to a restrictive covenant (the servient land). First, the benefit of a freehold restrictive covenant is not recorded on the title of the land in benefit. It may well be then that the owner of that land is unaware of the covenant. Second is the obvious but often ignored fact that the covenant not only needs to be enforceable – it needs to have a beneficiary who is prepared to enforce it.

There are then a number of courses of action that might be taken to modify or extinguish the covenant.

An insurance policy indemnifying the cost of 'any' claim under the covenant is the first port of call for the developer of land subject to such a covenant. If this is unavailable the developer may seek to identify the land in benefit of the covenant and approach the owner of that land for a release of the covenant or a variation that would allow the development to go ahead. Alternatively, and possibly as a last resort, they may take legal action to have the covenant modified or extinguished under section 84 Law of Property Act 1925 as amended. Today this requires an application to the Upper Tribunal Lands Chamber. The procedure for modification can be seen in the Upper Tribunal decision in *Martin v Lipton* [2020] UKUT 8 (LC).

Indemnity insurance is the preferred route. The following points are to be appreciated:

(1) Note that I said that this should be for 'any' claim. The insurer should, for a premium, insure against any claim from those claiming benefit of the covenant.

(2) The premium is usually a modest single payment. Frankly if it were not it would indicate that the risk was high and the insurer would not wish to insure against it.

(3) Any funding bank will insist that indemnity insurance is in place.

(4) Note that the insurer will not wish the developer to have approached any potential beneficiary as this may increase the risk of a claim.

I strongly suggest that approaching the owner of that land in benefit is not the first course of action. It is possible that just one party in benefit has been identified but there may be others. I recall a case where the developer had paid an amount of money to a company bearing the same name as the beneficiary of a restrictive covenant imposed in the 1920s. In allowing a claim made by the owner of the neighbouring property, the tribunal member acknowledged the payment to the company but noted (with some humour) that the company had been incorporated in 1973. Clearly it was not the beneficiary of the 1920s covenant. The developer should only consider approaching the owners of land in benefit if they simply cannot obtain an indemnity insurance for 'any' claim.

The developer may apply to the Upper Tribunal for modification or discharge of the covenant. There will be a significant cost in taking a case to tribunal. The case may rely on a substantial change in the neighbourhood due to the grant of planning permissions since the covenant was imposed. There may be other factors that prevent enforcement. The tribunal publishes the results of cases and I would certainly recommend reviewing some similar cases heard by the tribunal to establish any chance of success prior to taking any such action.

Indeed the developer should weigh up the costs and the likelihood of success. This may depend on the benefit that the covenant gives to those properties in its benefit.

12.7   Restrictive covenants under a building scheme

To understand the four concomitants of a building scheme of covenants one has to look at the case of *Ellison v Reacher* (1908) 2 Ch 374. For our purposes it is sufficient to know that a building scheme is created where a developer subdivides a site into separate lots and wishes each of the lots to be able to restrict the development of the other lots. For example, they may divide the site into one acre lots. The covenant might restrict development to one house on each lot thereby presumably making the neighbourhood more select. The problem facing the intending developer of any one of the lots is the clear fact that all other owners have to agree to the subdivision of the subject lot. It is most likely to be the case that none of the other lots have themselves been subdivided and so no precedent exists that could support an application for modification under section 84. The clear issue is that it only takes one of the beneficiaries to refuse consent to the proposal.

See also *Allen & Others v Veranne Builders* (1988) NPC 11, an Upper Tribunal case concerning the Wilderness estate in Sevenoaks, Kent.

12.8   Adverse possession

What are the implications when the developer views a site and sees that neighbouring owners have encroached onto the land? The important question that arises here is, has this occupation of the land given the neighbours the right to claim ownership of the land? Often if this were to prove to be the case it would have serious implications, for example if planning permission had been granted and could not be implemented due to the encroachment. The question in legal terms is: Is the occupation adverse possession?

Adverse possession is a term that really is what it says it is. The possession has to be adverse and it has to be possession. It is where someone who does not own land occupies it and subsequently claims ownership of it. Under the Limitation Act 1980 time runs against the owner of the land from the moment the land is adversely occupied. There has to be possession which is continuous and exclusive. That possession requires to be without force, without secrecy and without permission and with the intention to exclude the world at large.

Today, adverse possession of registered land is subject to the rules set out in Schedule 12 of the Land Registration Act 2002. The period of possession is reduced to 10 years from the 12 in Schedule 1 of the Limitation Act 1980 but the registered owner has to be notified of any claim thereby making it less likely that the claim will succeed. Such a notification is made by the Land Registry form B149. This states the claim including the title number, description and a plan showing the land which is claimed. Adverse possession of unregistered land remains in timescale subject to the Limitation Act 1980. (My view of this is that the draughtsmen of the 2002 Act saw an opportunity to have owners of unregistered land seek to register their land to benefit from the notification process).

I recall a claim made against land owned by my company. It had got to a point where the Land Registry were to issue a fresh title to the claimant who had occupied the land for more than the statutory period of 12 years under the Limitation Act 1980. He had, however, failed to take into account a letter sent to me by his solicitor confirming that he had permission to occupy the land. Under section 29 and section 30 Limitation Act 1980, that permission meant that the clock started running from his acknowledgement. His claim failed.

12.9   Boundaries
One must always bear in mind that the registry will do its best to show boundaries accurately but it issues the caveat that boundaries shown on plans are 'common boundaries' and thereby the exact siting of a boundary cannot be guaranteed. This has been the case since the Land Transfer Act 1897 but even modern plans cannot always show accurately the boundaries of a curtilage. Disputes as to the correct position of a boundary are all too common and are often decided by inspection on site by a boundary surveyor appointed by RICS.

The surveyor will inspect the title and other documents and consider witness statements. They will inspect the boundary and look for markings, fence posts and ditches and such to ascertain the true boundary.

12.10   Minor interests
Minor interests are those that are not registrable themselves as legal estates. They are entered into the register as notices, cautions, restrictions or

inhibitions. Examples of minor interests are third party rights over the land such as easements and restrictive covenants.

12.11   Overriding interests

These are mentioned above. They are rights that are binding notwithstanding they are not entered on the register. This is a curiosity given that a buyer might be unaware of such a right's existence. I have often thought this an odd position when one considers that an equitable right in property can be defeated by 'Equity's darling', the bona fide purchaser for value without notice (see *Pritchard v Briggs* [1980] Ch 338).

Some reductions in the scope of overriding interests have been introduced in Schedules 1 and 3 Land Registration Act 2002 but the developer should be aware of legal easements that have been documented but have not been entered in the register. I have only once confronted this anomaly which resulted simply in my connecting a neighbour's drain to the foul sewer laid on my new site.

12.12   Leases

A lease is a contract between a landlord and a tenant where the landlord grants a right to the tenant to occupy a property for a term of years. The right to occupy is subject to conditions which, given that the lease is made by deed, are known as covenants.

Tenancy agreement

This is a short term lease. Today the tenancy agreement most often encountered by the developer is the Assured Shorthold Tenancy introduced by the Housing Act 1988. This is the agreement whereby no fault eviction can be secured under section 21. It is anticipated that this may be modified going forward making eviction only possible for breach of the agreement under section 8. My own view is that this defeats the very object of the Assured Shorthold Tenancy and that no fault eviction should be retained.

Security of tenure

It has long been recognised that there is an imbalance in the positions of landlord and tenant; that is to say, it is easy to see how a landlord can hold all the cards in the landlord and tenant relationship. It used to be the case that a landlord could terminate a tenancy on any pretext. Statute has intervened to give tenants more rights and the right to continue in occupation of the property is security of tenure.

Security of tenure is simply whatever security exists in a tenancy agreement or by statute allowing a tenant to remain in occupation of premises. The acquisition of land may involve the acquisition of tenanted property and it is useful to be aware of the rights of tenants to security of tenure. It needs to be understood that different types of tenancy have different rights in terms of security of tenure. So the developer or project manager needs to be sure what kind of tenancy applies.

Succession rights
Succession rights are the rights of spouses and issue of the tenant to succeed to the tenancy upon the death of the tenant subject to their having been in occupation of the premises. Examples of statutory succession rights include agricultural tenants under the Agricultural Holdings Act 1986 and residential tenants under the Rent Act 1977.

While there are few examples of succession today, and the developer is unlikely to come across such rights, we should not assume that these rights have been consigned to history. Who knows? It is perfectly possible that legislation introduces the right of succession as a way of giving greater security of tenure to certain tenants.

One statutory security of tenure that very much exists today is the business tenancy. I once spoke with an excited young developer who was assembling a residential development site that had, within the mix, an existing commercial tenant. I was confidently assured that there was no problem with vacant possession as 'the lease is coming to an end'. Does this mean that vacant possession is assured? The answer is no, not necessarily. There are strict rules within Part 2 of the Landlord and Tenant Act 1954 relating to business tenants and the landlord's ability to obtain vacant possession upon expiry of a business lease. If the tenant wishes to remain in the premises it is not an automatic right for a landlord to remove them.

Here the developer is required to put forward a strategy to cope with such a situation. The starting point is the reasons why the landlord might oppose the grant of a new tenancy set out in section 30 of Part 2 Landlord and Tenant Act 1954. Indeed, the proposal to undertake redevelopment of the property may well be the reason why the tenancy might be terminated.

The developer should examine carefully the rules for terminating a tenancy and to be aware of the compensation to the tenant that this might incur.

12.13   Environmental law

Construction of a project may encounter aspects of environmental law. This is covered in statutes such as the Environment Act 1995 and 2021, Environmental Protection Act 1990 and Wildlife and Countryside Act 1981. Below I include soil contamination, wildlife habitats and protection of species, water aquifers and statutory nuisance.

Soil contamination

A soils report will generally need to be carried out to examine the bearing capacity of the subsoil for foundation design. The surveyor undertaking the survey will also take samples of the soil for analysis to reveal whether it is contaminated in any way. Examples of sites with potential for contamination might include petrol stations, tanneries or general industrial sites.

Wildlife habitats and protection of species

The principal legislation prohibiting and limiting actions involving wild animals and birds is the Wildlife and Countryside Act 1981. It should be noted that habitats of wild animals and birds are equally protected. Fines for contravention can be substantial and custodial sentences possible.

The Environment Act 2021 sets out long term targets for environmental improvement. Of particular relevance to development are the ambitions for waste and resource efficiency and recycling. The Act includes amendments to the Clean Air Act 1993 to improve air quality and water (Land Drainage Act 1991).

It is, however, the provisions to strengthen the duty on public bodies to conserve and enhance biodiversity including mandating a net gain biodiversity through the planning system that impacts on the developer.

The developer will therefore require an ecology report in support of their planning application. The ecologist will survey the site to identify the presence of certain species and identify biodiversity gains that could be achieved.

12.14   Hydrology

If a site for development is in or close to a flood plain then a Flood Risk Assessment will need to be undertaken to assess how the development can be carried out without the risk of flooding or in any event to mitigate the impact of flooding should this occur.

12.15 Noise

Construction sites are subject to limitations on the noise created. It makes sense that noise should be limited as much as possible and operations creating noise undertaken only in working hours.

12.16 Statutory nuisance

There is no definition of statutory nuisance. The nuisance complained of should either risk peoples' health or interfere with their enjoyment of land. Whereas an action in nuisance might be a civil claim, statutory nuisance can be subject to an action by a local authority (Part 3 Environmental Protection Act 1990).

12.17 Strict liability: The rule in *Rylands v Fletcher*

This is liability for damage that results from a landowner taking on to their land a non-natural use that escapes and causes damage to neighbouring property. In *Rylands v Fletcher* (1868) LR 3 HL 330, Rylands had constructed a reservoir and water escaped, but the damage could conceivably be, say, caused by chemicals escaping from being stored on a building site.

Case study 9
Restrictive covenant
Key Issue: Whether a freehold restrictive covenant can be indemnified.

Restrictive covenants expressed to prevent the construction of additional houses are all too common where perhaps a surplus parcel of land (Garden Plot) was sold for development subject to a restriction that say one house only shall be built on Garden Plot. The restrictive covenant is expressed to be for the benefit of the retained land with the intention of preventing overdevelopment of the Garden Plot to the detriment of the retained land.

There has been the ability to challenge restrictions of this kind. Section 84 Law and Property Act 1925 introduced a procedure for an application to 'modify' or 'discharge' a restrictive covenant where circumstances have changed the benefit that such a covenant will bestow, for example, where development has taken place on the land in benefit of the covenant. This application is today made to the Upper Tribunal Lands Chamber.

In this case the restriction was to the benefit of the land from which Garden Plot was taken (Two Acres) as its owner, the vendor of Garden Plot at that time remained in residence at Two Acres. As time goes on change inevitably occurs and Garden Plot becomes a site with potential for two houses.

The covenant is in benefit of Two Acres but now Two Acres has itself been redeveloped into five houses. Does the benefit of the restrictive covenant disappear or does it attach to each and every one of the five houses that occupy the land of Two Acres?

In the case of *Federated Homes Ltd v Mill Lodge Properties Ltd* [1980] 1 W.L.R. 594, it was held that the restrictive covenant was annexed to any part of the entire plot. So here, any one of the five owners of the houses on Two Acres could in theory enforce the covenant.

This makes the developer's position tricky. Do they go ahead with the acquisition of Garden Plot? What steps do they take to overcome the covenant?

First, we know that if planning permission is granted its grant could overcome a covenant such as this in an application under section 84 for modification or discharge of the covenant. Next, we know that in spite of the entry on the Garden Plot register referring to the burden of the covenant, its benefit will not appear on the titles to the five plots. We are also aware that the cost of defending an action under section 84 can be expensive and there will be a reluctance on the part of beneficiaries to incur such a cost. It will also be the case that if the proposed development is reasonable there will in any event be few objections.

Conclusion
An application for Garden Plot was made following consultation with the owners of the five houses on Two Acres. A restrictive covenant indemnity policy was taken out to cover any claims but this only indemnified if no claim was made prior to the construction reaching roof level. No claims were made.

Embarrassing admission
The developer proposing the development of Garden Plot was me. The developer of the five houses had also been me. In other words, I had at that time owned Two Acres completely oblivious of the covenant. Had I been aware of it I could have extinguished it when the land was in my ownership and saved the need to indemnify the risk of its potential subsequent enforcement against Garden Plot.

Case study 10
Easements
Key issue: Capacity of an easement.

We have seen that an easement is a right over the land of another, indeed often more accurately under the land of another, as it is for drainage or services.

Where an easement exists to benefit a 'dominant tenement' that is the site being acquired, will it be adequate to benefit the site when developed? Often the development, almost by definition, will increase the number of houses on the site. Where a sleepy bungalow existed in benefit of the drainage easement will the development of ten new houses still be able to enjoy that benefit?

Here I am not referring to the capacity of the drain, the physical pipe buried under the soil, but the legal right to use it for the ten new houses rather than the sleepy bungalow.

A number of legal cases have addressed this question. First, in *Jelbert v Davis* [1968] 1 W.L.R. 589, an access easement granted to accommodate agricultural land was used to accommodate the land when developed by 200 holiday caravans. Lord Denning held that the form of user was not relevant but that the volume of use was 'so extensive as to be outside the contemplation of the parties at the time the grant was made'.

In *Graham v Philcox* [1984] Q.B. 747, the enlargement of the dominant tenement had no effect on the easement 'so long as the character and extent of the burden was not excessive'.

In *Attwood v Bovis Homes* [2001] Ch 379, Bovis developed a housing estate on agricultural land that benefitted from an easement to discharge surface water. Could Bovis then rely on the easement for the housing development? It was likely to be an intensification of use. It was held that it could.

Chapter 13

Construction of the project

'A [person] with organisational skills can run a construction company without ever having picked up a hammer and nail.'
Warren Farrell

Developers are not always contractors undertaking the construction of their projects themselves. Many will hire a construction contractor to undertake all the construction work acting as the main contractor who hires the subcontractors. It is possible with the right organisational skills to run a development company without a full understanding of construction. The developer is not free from responsibility, however. Clearly, they will have to meet payment of the cost of the works to the main contractor usually against a monthly application submitted by the contractor's estimator. In practice many developers will understand the construction process sufficiently to set up important pre-requisite actions and maintain close inspection of the works as they progress.

13.1 Pre-build/start meeting

Whether the team is to undertake the construction work itself or the developer is appointing a main contractor, it is necessary to have a pre-build/start meeting to ensure a full discussion of the site issues that will arise during the course of construction and to ensure the communication of all information including schedules of works, drawings, specifications, planning restrictions, method statements and risk assessments and any contractual commitments to vendors or perhaps neighbours.

The purpose of a pre-build meeting is not only to plan the construction phase going forward but also to make the construction team aware of the overall project objectives including timescales, site acquisition constraints and obligations, collateral agreements, planning conditions and any other contractual obligations.

A pre-build meeting should also be a risk assessment of the project, an opportunity to identify risks to health safety and security. An agenda for such a meeting should incorporate the information enumerated below:

(1) Ownership of the site should be advised to the contractor or construction site manager if they are not aware of it. They should also be advised of

the personnel who will be visiting the site on behalf of the owner (the employer's agent) or the funder (the project monitoring surveyor).

(2) Schedule of works.

The contractor will expect to have a schedule of works clearly setting out what they are to build and often how they are to go about it.

(3) Who is the new homes warrantor and who will visit the site on their behalf? Often the building inspector will be responsible for reporting to the new homes warrantor but a separate surveyor may have been appointed and may indeed be inspecting on a more regular basis.

(4) A description of the site with an emphasis on the restrictions to movement into and across it such as sloping ground for machinery. Is the access limited for construction vehicles or is it shared with other vehicles? Are there any obstructions? Consider deliveries of materials, muck away and scaffold lorries and parking of operatives' vehicles.

(5) Confirm ownership of boundaries particularly where these are to be replaced or upgraded. Discuss what new fences have been agreed and when they will be erected. Is there a party wall surveyor and will they need to make inspections as work progresses? Who will notify neighbours of the start date?

(6) Consider security fencing and illumination. Are cameras likely to be necessary?

(7) Also understand how storage is to be made. This may well affect insurance.

(8) It will be important to ensure that reports and plans are passed to the site manager including any method statements.

(9) Consider any contractual issues such as subcontractor design that may require collateral warranties, or use of machinery on site that might require notification to the insurer.

(10) Confirm insurance of the works and insurance of any existing buildings on site.

(11) If a construction plan has been prepared to satisfy a planning condition, this will be a document that will need to be provided at the pre-build meeting. A waste management plan may form part of this but if not, it is worth a discussion as to how waste will be minimised and disposed of.

(12) Accommodation is an expensive cost on a construction site and is often underestimated. A construction site manager's hut, secure storage, canteen, drying room and WC are essential. Drainage and temporary electrics will need to be provided for site accommodation. Clearly the siting of accommodation is critical.

(13) Confirmation of services to the site operations and connection of services to the new buildings will need to be planned at an early stage.

(14) The developer will need to go through the planning conditions and their implications and ensure that site staff have a drawings schedule with references and dates that ensures they have up-to-date plans and specifications.

(15) List the main risks identified and the action to be taken to mitigate these risks.

(16) The contractor will issue the F10 notice to the HSE which is easy to do online.

13.2   Building contracts

The bank or funder will wish to see that the developer has instructed a reliable contractor and that a recognised construction contract will be entered into between the developer and the contractor. A Joint Contracts Tribunal (JCT) contract is often used for this purpose. Where the design is undertaken for the contractor, or the contractor is to continue responsibility for the design it is usual for a Design Build contract to be used. VAT on design fees is thereby zero-rated together with the construction works themselves for new work where a Design Build contract is signed prior to engagement of design consultants. Design Build contracts are also a 'one stop shop' for liabilities under the contract and it is always worth the developer considering engaging a contractor who will take responsibility for the design under such a contract.

The alternative will be to enter into a standard JCT contract with design instructed by the developer to independent architects and engineers.

Joint Contract Tribunal contracts

The JCT issues standard building contracts for use with construction projects. These are comprehensive and independent in that they do not favour one party or the other. There are many complex issues that arise in construction disputes, and it is reassuring to know that JCT contracts are well understood by expert quantity surveyors and lawyers and that a dispute may be swiftly resolved where the JCT contract has been adopted.

Collateral warranties

Collateral warranties are contracts collateral to a main contract. They create an obligation from design consultants who are not party to the main contract but may nevertheless be culpable if some aspect of the design were to fail. This obligation is usually to the funder but may, in some circumstances, be to a purchaser or tenant. In other words, they create a liability in contract between a party that may need to rely on the design consultant in the event of failure.

The developer may simply offer their funder a collateral warranty signed by their contractor company for the benefit of the funder. There is a standard form that goes with a JCT/DB contract. Some funders insist on collateral warranties from all contractors and consultants who are to provide any part of the design. Less often, some funders are happy that a contractor's collateral warranty is adequate when a Design Build contract is used.

I do not consider it necessary to require consultants to be responsible to purchasers and tenants for residential projects, but merely to the funder which is in practical terms merely for the duration of the project.

13.3   VAT

VAT on new build residential buildings for sale is zero-rated. Where subcontractors submit invoices for payment including VAT, the gross amount should be paid and the VAT claimed back from HMRC. Clearly the company engaging the subcontractors will need to be registered for VAT. I have already advised how I do this simply by having my own VAT registered construction company contracted to SPV development companies. The contractor is thereby responsible for invoices on the construction work and thereby reclaims the VAT.

VAT returns

New houses are zero-rated for VAT. It is therefore important for the construction company undertaking the construction to be registered for VAT.

Returns should be submitted on a monthly basis. In this way a refund of VAT is received each month.

Reverse charge
VAT reverse charge is an anti-fraud measure designed to counter sophisticated VAT fraud whereby a suppler can invoice with VAT and retain the VAT without paying HMRC.

Construction is one area where the VAT reverse charge applies. From March 2021, certain suppliers will invoice the contractor net of VAT so that the VAT is paid direct to HMRC.

13.4   Contract Sum Analysis
The Contract Sum Analysis (CSA) is the breakdown of costs allocated to each trade in a residential project.

Preparation of a CSA is a useful discipline. Where construction work is being let to a contractor, they will provide the CSA but where the developer is also the contractor this document should also be prepared and appended to the JCT contract. The funder will no doubt wish to see a copy of the building contract prior to commencement of works and may wish to see the CSA at that point. The CSA is used to value the cost of variations to the works. Drawdown of funding is often made against the figures in the CSA.

When preparing the CSA, it is important not to forget or underestimate the cost of temporary works, for example scaffold, crash decks, temporary surfaces for construction traffic, site accommodation, plant and equipment, and signage. It is equally important not to include non-construction costs such as fees and furnishings. The CSA should be the construction cost of the works.

13.5   Project programme
A programme of works will need to be drawn up for each project showing each trade and activity on site over the project period so that progress can be monitored. This usually takes the form of a horizontal bar chart on a spreadsheet with the date marked on the top line so that one can see which subcontractors are on site at any date in the programme. Project programmes can be very detailed. It is not necessary to go into too much detail for a small residential project but nevertheless essential to have some form of programme.

13.6   Construction management plan

A construction management plan is often required as a planning condition to give an idea of the impact the construction work will have on the location. Even if it is not, it is worth setting out a site layout showing site accommodation, parking, storage and service trench proposals as this will help subcontractors plan their works. If required as a condition of the planning permission, it may be necessary to consider additional site management issues such as hours of work, wheel washing, scaffold inspections and possibly a programme of works external to the site boundaries.

13.7   Main contractors

The main contractor enters into a contract to undertake the whole project hiring all subcontractors themselves and dealing with issues under the construction contract. They will arrange the insurance for the period until practical completion. They may arrange the new home warranties though I would expect this should be done by the developer. They are also the principal contractor for the purposes of the Construction (Design and Management) Regulations 2015 and they should be in a position to provide a written statement setting out the methods of construction.

The building contract will usually be a standard JCT so terms are set by an independent body. Often developers like to insist on a fixed price for the works. I caution that where a contractor is held to a price that is unrealistic this may be an incentive to reduce quality. A main contractor will no doubt work for several developers at one time so the developer should be sure to see that manpower is not spread too thinly. What can be a benefit is the main contractor's buying power due to scale and contacts. It is not always the case that a quotation from a main contractor is wildly in excess of the developer's contract sum analysis.

13.8   Subcontractors

If the developer is to be the main contractor and are themselves working with subcontractors the first thing that will strike them is how professional most are. This is possibly because they concentrate on one trade only and have thereby become experts in all matters concerning their trade. They are also able to advise on matters concerning their trade and it is always worth discussing the works with the subcontractors to benefit from their knowledge.

The developer/contractor will need certain information from subcontractors prior to making payments to them and it is a good idea to record this information well in advance of receipt of their first application for payment.

They need to know whether the subcontractor is working under the Construction Industry Scheme (CIS) in which case it will be necessary to make a deduction from the subcontractor's application for payment as shown by the application and submit this to HMRC on the 19th of each month when PAYE is due.

The developer/contractor will need a copy of the subcontractor's insurance to forward to their insurer.

The subcontractor will need to provide method statements for particular works that might be required, for example by the conservation officer to a listed building.

The subcontractor will also need to provide risk assessments in relation to the works they are to undertake.

For contract purposes I do not ask any more than that the subcontractor sign the terms and conditions prepared by me. Seeking the signature to a detailed JCT subcontract always seems to me to put subcontractors off tendering for projects.

Procurement

Procurement is the process of securing supplies and appointing subcontractors to the project to undertake the trades that are required. Clearly the number of subcontractors engaged will depend on the project's size and complexity. I generally find that for a small residential project some 25 to 30 separate subcontractors will be appointed. I advise that where possible the number of subcontractors should be limited as far as possible to avoid utilising time in organisation. This is done by ensuring that no unnecessary specialist trades are required on the project particularly on finishes at completion when funding is at its maximum.

When seeking tenders from subcontractors it is essential to describe as much as possible the scope of the works and to ensure that each subcontractor submits their bid in like terms. It is sometimes useful to compile a template for the tender so that the subcontractors all follow it, allowing an easy assessment of tenders when received. Those more complicated work packages will benefit from input from a quantity surveyor who will compile a template of works and may well have a list of subcontractors they have used before. Other work packages such as decoration will probably not require detail sufficient to require a quantity surveyor. Many specialist subcontractors will know exactly what the requirements are when looking at plans and itemise their tender in a professional manner that is easily understood.

Procurement tracker

The contractor will find it useful to have a procurement tracker which is simply a spreadsheet listing the trades and marking up in three columns trades that have been sent out for tender, responses and acceptances. They may wish to further add the name of the firm appointed to undertake the works and the sum quoted. The procurement tracker can then be referred to from time to time to ensure that nothing is overlooked.

Quotations

When seeking tenders, it is useful to have quotations from each subcontractor on the same basis. I have tried sending out a template to ensure this but in my experience subcontractors will ignore it and submit their quotation in their own way. It is then the project manager's job to compare like with like and spot works omitted from the price. This may involve checking dimensions as often assumptions are made that do not relate to reality, merely to reduce the tender price to be claimed later by way of variation. I generally go to three firms for each trade, but I do know that many contractors will go to many more to seek out the best deal.

Insurances

It is important that subcontractors have in place insurance that covers all the risks associated with their trade. This is generally dealt with in one annual policy to cover the works, public liability and employers' risks. It is important that such cover is in place and is recorded by the developer as not only will this allow a claim in the event of an incident but the developer's own insurer will require the developer to employ subcontractors who are themselves appropriately insured.

Retentions

A retention of some part of payment to a subcontractor until completion of the works is commonplace. The standard retention is 5%, split as to 2.5% six months from completion and a further 2.5% twelve months from completion. The purpose of the retention is to ensure that any defects in the work are remedied by the subcontractor following completion of their work. I dislike holding retentions and I prefer to trust subcontractors to undertake remedial work without them. Many subcontractors will give a better price if a retention is not held. Retentions make it difficult to close a job upon completion as an amount remains to be paid. However, it has to be acknowledged that the retention is held to ensure that subcontractors undertake remedial work where necessary.

13.9   Method statements

A method statement obliges one to commit to writing the procedure for carrying out a certain task. Many construction related activities can be dangerous if embarked upon without going through some form of plan and that plan may well highlight an issue or need for a certain piece of equipment that will make the task less hazardous. It is usual for subcontractors to provide evidence that they have done this.

13.10   Risk assessments

Many construction operations will require risk assessments identifying the risks associated with the trade. In my experience the risk assessments I have seen are of a wholly generic nature and not written for the project itself.

13.11   Subcontracts

The JCT does have subcontractor contracts to issue with its main contracts. For small scale works I do not use these. I find that most subcontractors prefer a less formal appointment. A letter referring to the quotation for the works, the personnel contacts, conditions and a copy of the relevant drawings is generally sufficient.

13.12   Site management

A construction site manager is a requirement on site at all times to satisfy health and safety law. An experienced site manager will pay for themselves by the saving they are able to make in time and methods. They will be available to supervise deliveries and storage, do take offs of measurements of quantities and order materials. They will make technical decisions such as ground levels and generally deal with the day-to-day running of the site. Small development sites may require a second pair of hands with a labourer undertaking general work and giving support to subcontractors.

13.13   Site address

This is an obvious point but one that it is necessary to make. It is surprising how many addresses a site can have. Land to the rear of Willow Close can be The Old Curiosity Shop, Main Road Greenville, Mrs Smith's garden and others. It is important that everyone uses the same name and it makes sense to address the site as the main entrance for construction vehicles.

Service companies will require a permanent address to connect their services to. The developer will have had to agree the official postal address of the development with the street naming authority well in advance.

13.14   Services
The developer will no doubt wish to supply a shared service trench on site so that water, gas, electricity and telecoms can be laid together. This will require organisation and patience. Usually the groundworker will undertake on site excavation work with service companies laying their pipes and cables in these excavations.

The service companies may require legal easements to be signed by the developer (landowner) prior to undertaking the work. This will apply to any third party land that the services will be crossing so the developer may need to agree easements with third parties. There may be rights of access over a private road but that does not necessarily give the right to excavate for services.

The developer should ensure that they record the route of services so that these can be supplied to buyers' lawyers and surveyors.

13.15   Signage
The site should be clearly sign posted to avoid delivery vehicles missing turnings into the access point to the site. The sign may give detailed health and safety information.

13.16   Drainage
Every site will need foul and surface water drainage. Surface water drainage may sometimes take place by soakaways on site, either shallow or deep bore depending on ground conditions.

If the site is at a lower level than the invert of the sewer it is to be connected to, then this can be dealt with by use of a submersible sewage pump connected to a rising main to the adopted sewer. In practice, a new manhole is placed near the adopted sewer to receive the site sewerage which is then delivered by gravity to the adopted sewer. This avoids back wash. It is common to install twin pumps to address temporary failure.

Connection to a sewer in the public highway will require approval from the waste water authority and a licence from the highway authority. In some cases a financial bond will be required to cover damage to the road that is held by the highway authority for a number of years. Some highway authorities may insist on an approved contractor from their own list to undertake these works.

13.17   Applications to funders

I suggest that valuations of ongoing works are undertaken at the end of each month. The works completed will be confirmed by the bank's monitoring surveyor upon site inspection against the pre-existing schedule they have drawn up. It is beneficial to the contractor to receive the maximum drawdown available to avoid delays. The PMS should therefore be made aware of unfixed materials on site (MOS), and advance payments to be made as deposits or pre-payment. It is of course useful to produce pro forma invoices for such payments. In this way the monitoring surveyor may be happy to confirm the fullest figure possible for drawdown.

Chapter 14

Health and safety in development projects

'Safety is no accident.'
A slogan

Construction sites rate high in the table of dangerous work environments and the developer has to be aware that they have obligations under the Construction (Design and Management) Regulations 2015 as well as those of the principal contractor. Indeed, it is as well for them to understand the requirements of health and safety as to do so will be essential if they carry out the construction work themselves but also helpful if they are employing a contractor to ensure that regulations are observed.

14.1 Construction (Design and Management) Regulations

The Construction (Design and Management) Regulations 2015 require that construction work is planned, risks identified, and information has been made available and shared. The construction phase plan is introduced by the regulations and so too a party named the principal designer.

Principal designer

The principal designer is not always the architect. It is the party who evaluates the risks in the design and its implementation. This might be a surveyor or project manager. Often there are aspects of the design that will be undertaken by someone other than the architect so I do not believe that it is always appropriate to appoint the architect as principal designer.

I believe that the role of principal designer is best carried out by the developer. It is they who have assembled and acquired the site, it is they who have appointed the consultants and made the decisions relating to the project. To fulfil this role, they will need to eliminate hazards and reduce risks of hazards where they cannot be eliminated. They should consider how the building will be cleaned, maintained and eventually demolished. They must ensure that the design of the workplace meets the Workplace Regulations 1992 and circulate all relevant information to the design team and the consultants. This is a relatively simple role if carried out conscientiously, many of the requirements of which are common sense.

Contractor's health and safety policy
The contractor will have a health and safety policy setting out the persons responsible for all matters relating to health and safety. A copy of this should be kept on site.

Principal contractor's plan
This plan will typically comprise of site health and safety files relating to all matters affecting health and safety for the project. It will be useful to maintain five separate files on site and to ensure that health and safety paperwork is collated, updated and readily available for inspection. I work on this basis with the following files.

File 1
Contract details.
Construction phase plan.
Principal designer plan.
Construction company health and safety policy.
Contract details and client details.
Details of Controls of Substances Hazardous to Health to be used on site.
Manual handling guidance
Working at height guidance.
Fire risk assessments.
Site diary.
Location of Accident and Emergency centre.

File 2
Subcontractors.
List of appointed subcontractors.
Letters of appointment.
Contact details.
Risk assessments and method statements.
Records of tool box talks.
Records of first aiders.

File 3
Insurance.
Principal contractors' insurance policy.
Consultants' insurances.
Subcontractors' insurances.
Hire insurance details.
Brokers advice on specialist works requirements and highlights of policy cover.

File 4

Planning.

Planning permissions and condition discharges highlighting restrictions on site operations that are conditions of the permissions.

Drawing index.

Drawings.

File 5

F10.

Inductions.

Permits.

Licences.

Construction phase plan

The construction phase plan relates to the project and should identify how the risks will be dealt with. I would expect to see the plan divided into the following schedules.

Schedule 1.   Team list, consultants and contact details.
Schedule 2.   Subcontractor's list and contact details.
Schedule 3.   Drawings index.
Schedule 4.   Terms and conditions of appointment.
Schedule 5.   Site rules.
Schedule 6.   Project programme.
Schedule 7.   Permits for hot works and excavations.
Schedule 8.   Record of permits and power tool and scaffold inspections.
Schedule 9.   Site register of inductions.
Schedule 10. List of first aiders.

If the contractor maintains files in this way they will have created a discipline that assists in avoiding accidents on site. What may seem like a lot of paperwork will, if updated rigorously on each project, become a useful source of site information.

Chapter 15

Services to and from the development

'What do we live for, if not to make life less difficult for each other?'
George Eliot

The availability of public services is one of the great benefits of living under the rule of law. Service undertakers are granted rights by statute to supply electricity, gas, water and telecommunications and to provide facilities for foul and surface water drainage. In return householders can rely on high levels of public health and the supply of services at prescribed costs and rates. Repair of these services is provided rapidly and efficiently such that users suffer minimal inconvenience. This is due to the ability of the service company to access third party land. Easements and wayleaves are the legal rights that allow services to cross private land. These are part of property law. This is something we take for granted but we should perhaps pause for a moment to consider what life might be like without the property law that gives us the ability to enjoy these services and what the possibilities would be for development without them. Examples of development that has taken place without these benefits abound in many parts of the world. In Kenya some 56% of the urban population live in slums. Kibera outside Nairobi houses some one million slum dwellers and is the largest slum settlement in Africa but certainly not the only one. These are informal settlements where there is no mains electricity, water or sewage disposal and disease, flooding and crime are rife. Crucially there is no system of property law to enable the provision of services in a fair and accessible way.

In this country the developer will require connections of all services to the new homes that they are having built. They will need to establish availability, though a lack of availability is more likely to be a lack of capacity of a service which may be upgraded but at a cost rather than a complete absence of service. The developer will therefore need to have made enquiries as to services and their capacity to serve their proposed development when they undertake their due diligence.

It is sometimes the case that the provision of services to the new homes will require a redirection of the existing arrangements for services to the site and that fresh easements may need to be secured across neighbouring land.

Negotiation of legal easements and the organisation of services can take some time to arrange so it is as well for this not to be left to the last minute when completed property is ready for sale.

15.1   Water services

The supplier of fresh water will be a water company appointed under the Water Industry Act 1991 as amended by the Water Act 2003. This Act requires the company to undertake any duty imposed under the Act and to exercise any powers granted under the law. The fresh water supply company may also be the undertaker responsible for drainage but this is not necessarily the case.

Public sewers

Foul sewers and surface water sewers are separate. There are very few examples of combined sewers and drainage authorities would not allow these today. It is therefore necessary for the developer to consider where connections to the public sewer system will be made for both foul and surface water sewers.

Foul sewers

The developer has the right to discharge drainage into a public adopted sewer. They will need to obtain consent of the drainage undertaker in order to connect to the public sewer or public lateral drain. This agreement is referred to as a section 106 agreement pursuant to section 106 of the Water Industry Act 1991 (not to be confused with section 106 of the Town and Country Planning Act 1990 which deals with planning obligations).

Surface water sewers

It is not always necessary to connect surface water drains to a surface water sewer. There are many cases where soakaways are acceptable. These can take the form of a shallow soakaway sited outside five metres from the building or a deep bore soakaway that takes surface water into the ground under the site. In some cases, there may be the opportunity to take surface water into a stream where one exists.

Pumped drainage

Where the ground level of a site is below the invert level of the adopted sewer then the drainage will require to be pumped up to a rising main. The foul must drain by gravity into the public sewer so that a rising main should discharge to a manhole that can then discharge by gravity into the adopted sewer. This requirement prevents back up. Submersible drainage pumps are a common feature of new developments and can be shared between a small number of dwellings or allocated to just one dwelling. These pumps can be used for both foul and surface water drainage.

15.2   Gas services

The Gas Act 1986 and Gas Act 1995 define gas companies as public gas transporters.

If a public gas transporter wishes to enter land to lay a new pipe without using compulsory purchase powers, it has to rely on negotiation with the landowner for an easement. The gas company is not likely to wish to exercise its compulsory purchase powers under Part 1 Schedule 3 Gas Act 1986 as this is a right to 'purchase' the land or rights. Such compensation would be assessed under the Land Compensation Act 1971 and is a costly and unnecessary procedure. This means that the developer will be required to enter into an easement with the gas company granting it the necessary rights to lay and maintain the gas pipe. The significance of this is the time required in dealing with the deed of easement. The developer should be aware that in arranging to lay the gas supply they will need to see that the easement is granted.

15.3   Electricity services

Electricity service is undertaken by UK Power Networks (UKPN) or specialist connection companies. This is not something undertaken by suppliers of electricity such as EDF Energy or OVO.

The benefit of using the statutory undertaker is their ability to make the connection to the existing supply which is often located in the highway.

15.4   Shared service trenches

It is possible that the construction team will wish to organise services such that a single trench is excavated for all services to be laid. The water is laid first and over it, gas and electricity. This ideal resolution can be straightforward if service companies cooperate in terms of timing. It can be extremely difficult to achieve where one service company delays and trenches are left open. One possibility is laying ducts for services such that the trench can be backfilled following the laying of the fresh water with the gas pipe or electricity pulled through the duct at a later stage. The best scenario is the organisation of the service companies to undertake their work in strict rotation.

15.5   Connection in the highway

Often connection to gas, water or electricity will be made in the highway. The developer should be aware of the location of the service in the highway as if it runs on the side of the highway opposite their development, the closure of the highway will need to take place. This can require a procedure that takes some time to arrange.

15.6   Connection to dwellings

The dwelling that is to be connected to an electrical supply has to be identifiable. That is to say it will have to be known by an official address and the developer will have had to agree this with the street naming department.

It is necessary to advise the undertaker of the location of the meter box on the external wall of the dwelling. Connection to the dwelling itself is then undertaken by the appointed electrician.

15.7   Clean energy

We are all aware that sustainability of energy sources has come into focus in recent years and the Future Homes Standard is a drive for new homes to produce 75% less carbon emissions compared to current standards by 2025. The effect on the development of new homes will require a change of emphasis moving away from carbon energy sources such as gas to clean energy generated on site where this is possible. Most LPAs insist on electric car charging points for new houses with parking areas and solar panels are sometimes required.

Chapter 16

Property taxes

'Taxes are the price we pay for civilisation.'
Oliver Wendell Holmes

The market economy supported by the rule of law comes at a price. Taxes allow governments to maintain the rule of law, a cost to pay for civilisation. Property is attached to land and buildings. It is the mind that operates the use of the land or building. Its details and those of its occupants are recorded at the Land Registry, polling records and other registers. Transfer of ownership has to be registered in a manner that shows the ownership on a public register and it has an official address. Property is often valuable and often a source of income by way of rents for those fortunate enough to own it. It is not difficult to imagine then that these attributes make property an attractive source of taxation for HMRC.

Understanding what taxes are likely to be incurred, and what obligations will be incurred to pay taxes in a development project is vital. It is no use a developer proceeding with the acquisition of property without realising exactly what Stamp Duty Land Tax will be payable upon completion of the purchase, or what Community Infrastructure Levy will be charged upon commencement of the project. The price they will pay for a project may be severely limited by taxes, levies, section 106 planning obligations and affordable housing obligations. In *Parkhurst Road Ltd v SSLG & Anor* [2018] EWHC 991 (Admin) the High Court rejected a claim by the developer that a local planning authority should have regard to market evidence in assessing bench mark land value for the purposes of a viability assessment. Value had to be assessed against affordable housing policies as set out in its local plan. If the developer had failed to do this then he had simply overpaid for the land.

16.1 Stamp Duty Land Tax

Stamp Duty Land Tax (SDLT) is paid by the buyer of property on the acquisition of property via their lawyer. Rates of SDLT vary according to the existing use and value of the property being purchased and do not relate to the project that is to be undertaken unless the project falls within the exemptions to the tax. Such exemptions can include housing association developments, custom and self builds. If the developer is buying the project through a company, which they almost certainly will be, there is currently an additional rate of 3% SDLT to pay where the existing use is residential.

There is a useful stamp duty calculator online that will provide a figure of SDLT applicable to a transaction (see https://www.tax.service.gov.uk/ calculate-stamp-duty-land-tax/#/intro). It should be noted that if any part of the existing use is commercial then the whole falls to be subject to SDLT at the commercial rate of 5%. This can be beneficial when compared to the residential rates currently applying to high end property.

16.2 Community Infrastructure Levy

Today many local planning authorities charge a levy ostensibly to contribute to community infrastructure incurred by development in the area. The Planning Act 2008 introduced the Community Infrastructure Levy (CIL) and the CIL regulations were issued in 2010. CIL is calculated according to a charging schedule prepared by the local authority the figures to which are updated to RICS inflation figures each year. The levy is calculated according to every additional new build gross internal square metre of floorspace that is being added by the planning permission granted. It is, therefore, important to ensure that existing buildings are measured for the planning application so that the area of these can be deducted from the assessment. These existing buildings have to have been in use continuously for 6 months within 3 years ending the day of grant of the planning permission. It is also important to refer to the RICS code of measuring practice to check the core definition of Gross Internal Area (GIA) as accuracy in completing these figures is critical. Penalties can be levied where forms are not submitted on time and a custodial sentence can result from deliberately false information.

The developer will need to submit an assumption of liability notice prior to commencement of development (Form 1). Often it is good practice to submit this with the application if possible. This will contain the address and planning reference of the development and a description of the development together with the name of the person liable for the charge. Prior to commencement a commencement notice (Form 6) must be submitted. Failure to do so will incur a surcharge. A CIL liability notice is then issued shortly after the planning approval.

If the residential development project includes social housing, there may be a claim for exemption or relief from CIL.

There are a number of exemptions from the CIL charge. Form 7 relates to a claim for custom and self-build exemption. Where a new home is to be occupied by its builder then the custom and self-build exemption can apply. It is important that this form and a commencement notice (Form 6) are completed and that acknowledgement has been received prior to commencement as to fail to do so may invalidate the claim for exemption (see *Shropshire Council v SSCLG* [2019] EWHC 16 (Admin)).

16.3   Capital Gains Tax

Capital Gains Tax (CGT) is paid on the disposal of property. It is calculated on the increase in value of the property from the purchase price but allowing for costs in enhancing or maintaining the property. Where CGT accumulates through the increase in the value of investment property held by a listed property company, it is possible to witness a share value of less than the combined value of the properties owned by the company. This is because the market has marked in the accumulated CGT that will have to be paid upon disposal. Development projects are not generally subject to CGT as they are subject to corporation tax from a trading company.

Private residence relief

Proceeds from the sale of one's principal private residence are not subject to CGT. The exemption applies to any part of a principal private residence and therefore if part of a garden is sold off for a development, the receipts for this will generally qualify as exempt. There is thereby a benefit to a developer in negotiating to purchase part of a private garden from a landowner as the intending vendor will receive the proceeds of sale without the requirement to pay tax. It is easy to see that where a homeowner moves house on a regular basis, having undertaken considerable improvements to each house, there is the opportunity to benefit from tax free gains. HMRC will however be alert to those who 'trade' private residences in order to capitalise on this exemption and they may question the exemption where this is exploited.

16.4   Planning obligations

Planning obligations derive from section 106 Town and Country Planning Act 1990 as amended by the Planning and Compensation Act 1991. Indeed, they go back further. The development charge was a feature of the 1947 legislation which was repealed in 1954.

Section 106 Town and Country Planning Act 1990 substantially re-wrote section 52 of the former Act to introduce planning obligation agreements. The idea of these agreements is to impose obligations, restrictions and arrangements that go beyond the enforcement capability of planning conditions. As planning conditions, such 'obligations' may be challenged as ultra vires but as section 106 they become enforceable and indeed are registered as a local land charge. The significance of the section 106 here is that it is often an obligation to pay money as a contribution to secure planning objectives. An interesting feature of planning obligations is that the developer can propose them. Most commonly a developer will propose that part of a site will be commuted to the local authority in exchange for planning permission being granted for another part. In other words, the developer can, by use of a section 106 obligation, offer a 'deal' to the LPA to secure some public benefit.

16.5   Inheritance tax
Inheritance tax (IHT) is charged on the value of the deceased estate valued on the day before death, that is to say, excluding the effect that death may have had on that value. It is invariably a tax on property as a valuable estate will most often incorporate property.

It is also a motivation for the sale of property as executors may well find themselves having to pay the tax prior to the disposal of property forming part of the estate. Probate is the legal process that describes the dealing with assets of the deceased estate and thus property resulting from such an estate is often referred to as probate property. An application for probate is made to the Probate Registry by the lawyer appointed by the executor to confirm that the executors can deal with the estate.

While IHT is not a tax payable by the developer it is as well that they understand the motivations of an executor vendor when buying property.

16.6   Corporation tax
Corporation tax is charged for each accounting year on the profit made by a corporation as shown in its accounts. A corporation is a limited company which is most often the vehicle used by the developer to carry out the development project.

16.7   Income tax
The developer employing staff will need to deduct income tax from staff salaries as PAYE and pay this to HMRC. The developer's accountant will employ a specialist to calculate PAYE due and it is as well for them to employ the accountant to undertake this monthly calculation. Payment of PAYE is due by the 19th of the month following payment of salaries and will be made along with payment of CIS deducted from labour only subcontractors.

16.8   Construction Industry Scheme
The contractor has a duty to deduct tax from labour only subcontractors such as carpenters, and pay this to HMRC. The subcontractor will show

on their invoice the amount of labour and the amount of any material they have supplied and a calculation of how much is to be deducted under the Construction Industry Scheme (CIS).

16.9   Value Added Tax

New homes built for sale are zero-rated for Value Added Tax (VAT). That means no output VAT is charged on the sale price. It also means that input tax can be reclaimed on certain supplies invoiced to the business with VAT added. These are supplies related to the construction of the project and therefore should be invoiced to the developer's construction company. The reverse charge VAT scheme has, since March 2021, introduced the concept of the subcontractor paying the VAT direct to HMRC.

It should be noted that refurbishment of dwellings is not zero-rated and thereby VAT at standard rate will apply. There are currently reduced rates of VAT applying to buildings converted from commercial use to residential use.

16.10   Annual tax on enveloped dwellings

This tax is not relevant to developers but I include it for completeness. It is an annual tax on the value of residential property held for the benefit of a connected person and not let at arms length on the market.

16.11   Council tax

Council tax is levied by local authorities upon the value of hereditaments (individual properties) according to the 'band' the value of the property places it in. The council tax band was determined as at the last valuation date which was 1 April 1991 in England. The property is valued *rebus sic stantibus*, i.e. 'as it stands now'.

Upon issue of the practical completion certificate for a dwelling house, the building inspector will notify the council tax authority. Liability for council tax is incurred one month thereafter. That means that, in addition to paying for services and maintenance of a completed house while it remains unsold, the developer is also paying council tax.

I have not attempted to go into detail about each tax and indeed the reader will be aware that the levels of taxation and the rules that apply change from time to time. It is important, however, for the developer to consider the implications of various taxes when analysing a project in property.

Chapter 17

Marketing and sales

'Build something 100 people love, not something 1 million
people kind of like.'
Brian Chesky

The sale of a property is the exit from the development that creates the income to the developer. It will allow the developer to repay any bank or lender from the proceeds of sale. It will hopefully be at a value that gives a profit. It is therefore a most important part of the development process. The legal completion of the sale of the completed house or flat fulfils one of property's essential characteristics: the transfer of property from one owner to another.

A transfer of property will be by deed and undertaken between lawyers acting for each of the parties to the transfer. To achieve this transfer, lawyers will need to be sure of the ownership of title which will be registered rather than unregistered, and be prepared to add any fresh covenants and easements to that title that are necessary to give effect to the use of the building, and any indemnities needed to the developer regarding future liabilities. The title will, following transfer, be registered at the Land Registry in the name of the buyer.

The developer has to be conscious of the market for their product just as the supplier of any goods. They will have undertaken a market appraisal by way of a sales survey prior to committing themselves to the project. Their funder will have commissioned a report and valuation on the project which will have contained an analysis of anticipated sales figures. They will thereby have an idea of the likely sales prices for the development and the asking prices they will instruct their agent to seek.

Before instructing their sales agent there are matters they may wish to address.

17.1   Site naming

The naming of the development may seem slightly trivial compared to other matters to be dealt with. Street naming is, however, a feature of property in that the identification of an official address is an essential prerequisite to the registration of the property. The connection of utilities will only take place to an official address and the issue of the final certificate from the building inspector will need to identify the property by its official address. The official address of a property is then an essential part of 'the rule of law'. The ability of its occupants to obtain credit, the registration of the owners or occupiers of the property for local services such as health and education, and of course the ability of the state to identify owners and occupiers for local and national taxation will depend on it. It is not only the sales team that will wish to know the name of the development for their glamorous sales brochures.

The registration of official addresses is a process that can take some time to eventuate so it needs to be done as soon as possible. The developer will be asked to submit suggestions for a street name to the local authority street naming department. The department's role is to consult with the fire brigade and Post Office to see that there is no duplication of addresses in the local area that would cause confusion or even endanger lives where emergency vehicles go to the wrong address. This may mean that the local authority returns to the developer for an alteration to the proposals, often suggesting a name themselves which, in my experience, will always be something ghastly. My advice is therefore to consider the street name and submit suggestions early in the project's process rather than leave it to the point of sale.

17.2   Websites and social media

I have known many very successful developers who do not have websites. I cannot therefore say that they are essential but it seems to me that a website is the first port of enquiry for landowners, bankers, professional consultants and buyers. I would suggest that a good website can add credibility to residential development projects and those undertaking them. There is the opportunity to display current and past projects and to say something about the team's experience. Increasingly there is also the potential of inviting investment into projects. Developers are fortunate in requiring only a 'poster' style of website rather than an expensive interactive one for e-commerce.

It goes without saying that a website should be as glamorous as possible with attractive photographs. It should not be misleading and not over do the information. I refer buyers to the selling agent of each project that is listed. Videos and blogs are recommended by our marketing professionals to add life to a website and to keep it current. Various social media can be used to spread the word. I particularly like Instagram which I note as being popular with many smaller developers.

17.3   Selling

It is often said that there are two points at which one can sell development properties; off plan before the project has started building and when the project is complete. The period in between these windows of opportunity is more tricky as one is attempting to sell a building site which is unlikely to appeal to buyers and indeed a constant stream of viewers is likely to be a headache for those involved in the construction process. I am not sure whether this is entirely true as I have certainly sold during construction but generally in response to an agent's request to show around a specific buyer who has shown interest.

17.4 Selling off plan

How we all wish that we could sell everything off plan. Early exchanges of contracts give restful nights in the knowledge that buyers will move into our new homes when they are complete. I would always advise giving an agent the opportunity to sell off plan even if that merely involves contact with a shortlist of buyers. Just one early sale can provide confidence in the entire project, not just in the market but with the lender too.

There are potential downsides to off plan sales that should be considered. First is the potential to have sold at a low figure on a rising market such that on completion the property is considered to be worth more. Also there is the possibility that should the project suffer delays the buyer may pull out if their contract expires. They certainly will if the market has fallen during the project period.

Another downside is that a buyer off plan may well see the opportunity to revise plans and specifications. That is acceptable if they make decisions in accord with the construction process but often buyers are unable to see the consequences of changes made while construction is progressing. The rule here is get paid for alterations and extras prior to making them. In my experience, the buyer will typically be happy to pay for the change but will argue the cost consequences of the change. That is to say, they will be quite happy with payment for the additional kitchen cabinets but will question the cost of delay and moving the power points. If possible, the developer should carry out the project as planned with no alterations.

One potential benefit to an off plan sale is the ability to receive the deposit rather than have it remain in a solicitor's account. Any deposit will likely go to the lender as they have the right to require funds and the new home warranty will need to indemnify the buyer against the developer failing to complete the project. However, it will have the effect of reducing the borrowing and hence interest charged.

17.5   Selling on completion of the development
The more logical point at which to sell the project is on its completion. When the project is complete the developer is in a position to review all the information and to ensure that they are prepared for buyers. Here the potential difficulty arises when a buyer suggests that if only certain amendments had been made they would have been interested to buy. The developer then has to be confident that they have made the right choices of design and specification. It is also the case that upon completion of the development the bank loan is fully drawn and interest charges are at their peak. A completed development without sales is thereby a very scary thing for a developer and will have them wishing that they had sold some of the project off plan.

17.6   Sales brochures
I cannot recall how many brochures have been produced for the development projects I have been involved in. Many of these were glamorous deliberately to show off the company as much as the project. Probably the majority were thrown away before they were all distributed when the project sold. Today, developers rarely produce brochures – instead the buyer can download sales particulars from the agent's website. Where brochures are produced it is of course essential that they are accurate in the information that they provide as any misleading information can be challenged.

17.7   Show houses
Show houses are very expensive and require not only furniture and curtains but the gardens will need to be planted lushly and maintained to be immaculate. Show houses need to be fault free. Viewers have an uncanny habit of descending on the one unfortunate design feature or poor finish. However, sometimes when the market is tough, it will be necessary to fit out a show house, and it is a project in itself. The first rule is to identify the likely buyer. The developer may have already discussed this with the agent and kitchen supplier and chosen wall tiles and finishes to suit the buyer they have identified but now they will need to seriously consider selecting furnishings.

They must not yield to prejudices. Old people do not necessarily want to be told that they qualify for a wing back armchair. The developer should choose an interior designer who is able to explain how their approach meets the requirements.

17.8   Estate agents
I am a fan of estate agents. That is to say, the good ones. My point is that a good estate agent can save time and money and I cannot tell you how

many times I have been grateful to an agent for his or her expertise. I would always use a local agent, bringing in a second agent perhaps if the project is not selling and generally choosing a larger agent, not a second local agent who will merely duplicate what the first has been able to do. I would never just use the cheapest agent. I would therefore expect to pay between 1% and 1.5% commission, a figure considerably less than a few years ago when some agents were charging 2.5%. I consider it reasonable for an agent to charge an additional amount for brochures and certain advertisements where the developer has approved them.

I insist on a designated negotiator who I can speak to at any time rather than be passed around the office to hear different versions of the sale from different people. A weekly report on the sales is useful especially where several properties are being sold. It need only be a very brief update. I cannot understand why some agents do not provide this.

Sole agent

This is the usual arrangement for selling a new development. A sole agent has often been consulted earlier in the project and given advice as to finishes, and sale prices and the market generally. They will speak with intending buyers before the project is released for sale and identify buyers who are likely to be interested. In this way there will be a number of interested buyers ready to view when the project is released for sale. I like to appoint a sole agent as it saves duplication of instructions and a relationship can be built up.

Joint sole agent

One would be right to be suspicious of this term as it does not seem to me to make sense. If I am making little progress with my sole agent then I may instruct a second agent but I will be sure not to instruct the original and new agent in a way that allows them to share commission. It surely has to be winner takes all or the instruction of a second agent seems to me to be a pointless exercise.

Multiple agents

This is the arrangement where the seller simply instructs any agent who shows an interest to act for paying commission only to the successful agent. It should be noted that if agents are acting on this basis they will invariably charge a higher commission rate. It is unusual to work on this basis with a development project as the agent/developer relationship is perhaps more important and detailed than with an established house sale.

Estate agents are subject to the Estate Agents Act 1979 which regulates their activities and procedures. Among the requirements of estate agents is disclosure of interests in property they are offering for sale, transparency of fees and costs and the need for client approval of terms. The Consumers, Estate Agents and Redress Act 2007 suggests that all agents in UK should belong to an approved redress scheme dealing with complaints about the buying or selling of property.

In addition, estate agents are obliged to check clients' proof of ID before accepting instructions and record their check.

17.9 Mortgage valuation upon sale

A valuation will be carried out by a chartered surveyor on behalf of the bank providing mortgage finance to the buyer. The surveyor will examine the structure of the building and identify remedial work that needs attention prior to completion of the sale. They will confirm their valuation of the property and will be instructed to advise the lender whether incentives have been offered in order to secure the sale. The developer will have to complete a Council of Mortgage Lenders (CML) form declaring any incentives and give this to the chartered surveyor upon their inspection. The CML is now part of UK Finance.

17.10 Lawyer

On sale of new homes the developer's lawyer will require a great deal of information to be provided by the developer to satisfy the buyer's lawyer and any mortgagee.

Instructing a lawyer upon the sale of completed property requires unambiguous instructions as to what is to be achieved. The lawyer rarely views the site and it is important that the sale is described in detail together with what is required of the lawyer as mistakes can easily be made by assumptions. Important points will be the boundaries of the plot to be sold, its curtilage and ownership, the common parts of the site and what easements are to be granted over those common parts for the benefit of the plot to be sold. Conversely, any easements to be reserved over the plot to be sold for the benefit of retained plots need to be identified. If the project comprises private areas enjoyed by all plots then a service charge to cover communal electricity, repairs and landscaping for example will need to be referred to in the sale documentation with a requirement to commit the buyer to pay that service charge.

A full list of documents is set out below. Some points to consider with these are:

(1) A plan outlining the boundaries of curtilages of each home to be sold in red. It would be a disaster to complete the sale of the first plot only to find that the transfer had conveyed land that was planned to be included in the common parts or another plot. I once came across a developer who had sold a bicycle store destined for use by all buyers to just one of the buyers. Care must be taken to ensure that the area outlined in red is accurate.

(2) A schedule of details setting up a residents' company for onward maintenance of common parts and communal areas. This should identify the common parts, for example estate roads, drainage pipes and pump, visitors car parking and landscaping areas. I always identify for the sake of good order areas excluded from the common parts which are to be retained by the developer to avoid any misunderstanding at a later stage.

(3) A schedule of service charge contributions from each new home owner to the residents' company. I generally charge service charges to each GIAm^2 so that larger homes will pay more than smaller homes. Shares in the residents' company granted to each buyer will, however, be equal and the rights and responsibilities of maintaining common parts following completion of the development passed to them equally.

(4) The plan should show sight lines to the highway and reserve any necessary rights for these sight lines from the property on the frontage of an estate for the benefit of the estate road.

(5) The developer will know the site better than anyone. It is for them to ensure cross easements between the properties are in place such that all new home owners have rights over common parts and adjoining properties if required.

(6) A seller will be required to complete property information forms. It is important that this is honestly and accurately completed as any misinformation may invalidate the sale and allow a disgruntled buyer to require compensation. Cases that come to light under this heading usually involve disputes with neighbours that have not been reported on the property information form. For this reason, it is always advisable to avoid any disputes with neighbours to the site.

17.11   Sale plans

Sale plans are attached to the contract and will be used by the buyer's lawyer for searches in respect of the property. Upon completion they will be attached to the transfer and need to be submitted by the buyer's lawyer to the Land Registry to register the property in the name of the buyer. It is vitally important then that the plan shows accurately the property being sold and areas of common parts over and under which the rights of access and services applies. The Land Registry insist that plans are to scale, and have a North point marked on them. The plan will also be used by the buyer's lawyer for searches so it is a priority to have this prepared in readiness of sales. Some lawyers prefer registration of lots to be sold to be made prior to completion of the sale by the developer's lawyer to avoid complications following completion.

17.12   Deposits

Agents will usually obtain a commitment from an intending buyer by holding an initial deposit of a few thousand pounds. This deposit will in actual fact generally be held by the solicitor acting for the developer. If the buyer does not go ahead the deposit will be returned to them less any genuine expenses incurred by the developer. Upon exchange of the contract of sale, a deposit of 10% of the purchase price of the property will be paid to the developer's solicitor. This contract deposit is not returnable unless the sale does not complete as the long stop date in the contract is expired and the buyer wishes to exit the deal. The contract deposit is generally held by the developer's lawyer as stakeholder rather than being paid to the developer. It is possible for the contract deposit to be held by the lawyer as agent for the seller thereby allowing it to be paid to the developer but in many cases where there is bank funding, a contract deposit held as agent will need to be paid to the bank.

17.13   Sales information to be provided or available on sale of new home

Upon sale of a new home there are a number of documents that will need to be supplied to the lawyer which may duplicate those given to the buyer under the consumer code. Hopefully these will have been entered onto Dropbox to make transmission easier. These will mainly be required prior to exchange of the contract for sale.

(1)   Site description sheet: Legal sale plans with sale property edged in red, common parts in blue and boundary ownership marked by T marks.

(2)   Completed property information form and new home form from lawyer.

(3)   Historic and current planning permissions and condition discharges.

(4) Tree preservation orders (Part VIII Town and Country Planning Act 1990).

(5) Copy of section 106 Agreement of Planning Obligations (section 106 Planning and Compensation Act 1991).

(6) Evidence of CIL payments made (Community Infrastructure Levy Regulations 2019).

(7) Evidence of council tax banding and payments. This may not be available prior to exchange.

(8) Documentation relating to highway agreements including section 38 estate road adoption and crossover agreements under section 278 Highways Act 1980.

(9) Drainage authority agreement for sewer connections (section 106 Water Industry Act 1991).

(10) Confirmation of street name, numbering and postal addresses with postcodes from street naming authority.

(11) Initial notice of appointment of approved building inspector (The Building (Approved Inspectors etc.) Regulations 2010).

(12) Building regulations plans approval.

(13) Building regulations final certificate (section 51 Building Act 1984).

(14) Buildings insurance contractor's all risk or property insurance policy.

(15) Predicted EPC or final EPC.

(16) New homes warranty cover note.

(17) Gas safety certificate.

(18) Electrical installation certificate.

(19) Appliance warranties. Generally upon completion.

(20) FENSA certificates/guarantees doors and windows.

(21) Timber infestation guarantees.

(22) Boiler installation guarantee and heat loss factor.

(23) Flat roof guarantee.

(24) Solar panel MCS (Microgeneration Certification Scheme) certificate.

(25) Council Mortgage Lenders disclosure form.

(26) Management company documentation: Certificate of Incorporation.

(27) Service charge budget or planned maintenance schedule.

(28) HETAS certificate (solid fuel burner).

(29) Sound test and air pressure test.

(30) Site plan with North point and T marks with plot outlined in red, to scale for registration.

(31) Floor plans. It is as well to provide planning drawings rather than working drawings.

(32) Foul drainage pump certificate.

(33) Fan flow test.

(34) Certification of window and door locks (Part Q Building Regulations).

(35) Fire risk report generally where flats exit to communal areas served by smoke extractor.

(36) Confirmation that reference to Community Infrastructure Levy has been removed from the Land Charges Register.

It is a good idea to run through this list prior to exchange of a contract for sale to be sure not to miss anything.

17.14   Residents' companies

Certain developments will have common parts, areas and facilities within the development such as shared foul water pumps, landscape, car parks, private estate roads, entrance gates and amenity areas. If there is electricity supplied to the common parts of a development, a management company will need to be set up to collect maintenance payments from residents and pay the electricity bills. The developer will, in such circumstances, need to arrange a separate landlord's supply when arranging services connections to the development. If there is to be a residents' company it may be useful to use it for other matters. For example, the developer may confer the benefit of restrictive covenants limiting alterations of a group of houses to the land forming the communal parts. In this way the residents' company will have to approve any alterations proposed by neighbours which some buyers will find attractive. The developer will need to provide a schedule for contributions to the residents' company from each of the houses generally known as a service charge schedule.

17.15   Service charge schedule

It is usual to prepare an initial service charge schedule for the management company breaking down the expenditure that will be incurred by it in managing the common parts. These will include repair of shared surfaces, electricity for shared lighting, gates and sewerage pumps, garden maintenance and insurance. It is entirely the choice of buyers whether they continue to pay these service charges when the development is sold but it is useful to give an idea of what these costs might be. I calculate the contributions based on the net area of each property in the development and I always undertake to pay the service charges ascribed to unsold property.

The contributions to the residents' company in the service charge schedule should not be overestimated. Some buyers may be put off if they think that there is to be a large annual sum to be paid for maintenance.

17.16   The consumer code

The consumer code is a set of rules devised by the new home warrantors to ensure fairness, transparency and consistency in the service housebuilders give to buyers.

The code is distinct from the new home warranty itself and relates to the service provided to the home buyer rather than the house itself. The information to be provided to the buyer is to ensure that the buyer is properly informed and not misled as to what they are buying. Agents' details should present the property accurately and deposits have to be lodged with an independent party. A sturdy folder might be presented to a buyer on completion including electrical certificate, gás safety certificate, EPC, plan showing routes of services, brochures of fittings and names and addresses of suppliers. Details of dispute resolution should be included so that redress is available where the housebuilder fails to provide information or a service. The code is applicable during the defects period which is usually two years from the date of legal completion.

Completion of the final sale will yield the profit of the project with all borrowing paid back if the project has been carried out successfully.

Case Study 10
Sales
Key issue: A tale of the unexpected.

Being presented with an unexpected issue when selling a completed house can be a horror story. In this case a house was constructed close to a railway tunnel. The development involved demolition of an existing house and erection of a larger new house on the plot. The plot was not next to the tunnel but one removed, and the existing house had been constructed on brick foundations. The problem arose as the foundation of the new house was laid deeper than the existing house it replaced. The existing house had not experienced any vibration from the tunnel but the new house was subject to vibration when a train entered the tunnel. It was suggested that rock underlying the plot was conducting the vibration which was more of a tremor noticeable when the house was silent.

The issue was further compounded by defamatory remarks made by a local estate agent about the 'house that shakes'.

Conclusion
There is only one solution one can prescribe in such circumstances. Bank interest will roll up on a large detached house of this kind very rapidly and therefore the developer must sell the house quickly. They will therefore need to reduce the selling price even if this means a loss on the project. They can make their profit on the next project. In this case the estate agent who made the defamatory remarks about the house ceased doing so when instructed to sell it.

Chapter 18

Building projects to let

*'Real estate is an imperishable asset, ever increasing in value.
It is the most solid security that human ingenuity has devised.
It is the basis of all security and about the only indestructible
security.'*
Russell Sage

Here again is a quotation that recognises the distinction of property and land and buildings. The latter are indeed perishable, but property is the basis of all security.

The developer may not be wishing to sell the houses or flats they have built but to retain them and let them out in order to benefit from a rental income and any increase in the value of the property.

Build to let is becoming increasingly popular with large institutions and I believe it to be a reliable asset class. Unlike buy to let of existing property, the developer will have had the opportunity to incorporate a specification that suits their own letting model, making it easier to manage or more appropriate to the tenants they are aiming to attract. For example, I know of one build to let company that sets out three principles in their design: corridors and lifts of a size that can easily accommodate the frequent moving of furniture, bedrooms that are of similar size to appeal to sharers and communal heating systems where services are invoiced by the block manager so that frequent changes of customers do not require to be notified to the service companies, saving the endless paperwork only service companies are capable of.

It is possible to create a specification that incorporates durable finishes and fittings designed for ease of regular maintenance. A build to let portfolio of homes can have an identical specification in each home making replacement of fittings easily identifiable, interchangeable and readily available.

The developer who builds to let takes a financial risk in providing new homes. They calculate a design to suit the market and provide them to a standard required by a building inspector, new home warrantor and their prospective tenant. The provision of new homes is a benefit to the community and the developer has enlisted expertise in that provision. They will no doubt also have a mortgage on the properties and will anticipate the repayment and interest of these mortgages to be covered by the rent. They will also be responsible for the management of the properties going forward.

18.1 Residential tenancies

Without getting into too much detail it is only necessary for me to say that there are a number of residential tenancies in English law that have evolved over the years, most of which are not relevant to the build to let business. It may, however, be useful to understand the terms.

Secured tenancies

This is the public tenancy between council and tenant which has been subject to the Right to Buy introduced famously by Prime Minister, Mrs Thatcher, originally in the Housing Act 1980.

Demoted tenancies

These were introduced by the Antisocial Behaviour Act 2003 and created by a court order. They are usually 12-month tenancies where eviction is mandatory in the event of a breach.

Introductory tenancies

These are probationary public tenancies usually for 12 months.

Protected tenancies

Protected tenancies were introduced by the Rent Act 1977. This was the default contractual tenancy until 15 January 1989, the commencement date of the section of the Housing Act 1988 which created the Assured Shorthold Tenancy. Under the protected tenancy the tenant had security of tenure and there are succession rights to spouse and family. The rent had to be registered and fixed by a rent officer and is usually at less than market rent.

Regulated tenancies

This type of tenancy was introduced by the Rent Act 1977. It is simply the continuation of the protected tenancy upon its expiry or where succession has taken place to a spouse or family member living at the property upon the death of the statutory tenant. The regulated tenancy is subject to restricted rent fixed by a rent officer but there are no succession rights.

Assured tenancies

These were introduced by the Housing Act 1988. They give tenants a high degree of security of tenure and are most often used by housing associations.

Tenants can only be removed for breach of tenancy conditions under grounds for possession under Schedule 2 of the Act.

Assured Shorthold Tenancies

The Assured Shorthold Tenancy (AST) was created by the Housing Act 1988 as a way of giving landlords an opportunity to invest in residential property with a view to letting it out on commercial terms and a limited security of tenure. The term usually adopted is either 6 months or 12 months and the rent is market rent as agreed between the landlord and tenant often advised by a letting agent. Following the agreed term, 2 months notice may be given for possession. This is a section 21 notice, sometimes called a no fault eviction.

It can be seen that 15 January 1989 was a significant date for residential letting. A new form of tenancy had come about that was to expand the private rented sector of the property market from about 8% in 1979 to the 20% it is today. Private lettings had been made unattractive by legislation that limited rent and subscribed security of tenure obligations on landlords. Now, legislation offered the opportunity for landlord and tenant to agree a simple short let for residential property. The next few years saw financial institutions formulating buy to let mortgages and investors buying small flats and houses in preference to investing in pensions. Individuals on short term contracts away from home could rent a small flat rather than being restricted to hotel accommodation. It was a welcome shift in policy that has served us well.

Licences

A licence is not a tenancy. One feature of a licence arrangement is where the occupier does not have exclusive possession, for example, where a number of people share a house which is also lived in by its owner. It follows that under such an arrangement there is no security of tenure. The court will always look at the nature of the agreement rather than merely a document that purports to be a licence. A full explanation can be found in the House of Lords case of *Street v Mountford* [1985] A.C. 809.

18.2   Letting agents

Private letting has been a growth industry and a business I imagine most welcomed by many residential estate agents who, having avoided the complexities of surveying and valuation of property, have created lettings departments to supplement income derived from an increasingly more complex and protracted sales process. Letting agents have had to understand changing tenancy legislation and the legal requirements of letting a home. This has enhanced the professionalism of an area of the property business and lettings departments of some major estate agents now contribute substantial revenues to the business.

Letting agents' services

The services of the letting agent can merely be the introduction of a tenant and the execution of a signed Assured Shorthold Tenancy agreement, or a full management service.

Full management

A full management service implies the agent setting up the tenancy will ensure the tenant has acceptable references and will comply with the terms of the tenancy. The service will also ensure that the premises are kept in good repair, if necessary engaging trades to undertake repairs.

Rent insurance

In certain circumstances you can insure the payment of rent. This is clearly subject to a tenant credit check and usually only available where the letting agent is undertaking a full management service. It does, however, give a guarantee to the landlord that they will receive their rent.

Tenancy deposit protection schemes

There is a statutory requirement (Tenant Fees Act 2019) for tenants' deposits to be lodged with an approved tenancy deposit protection scheme. This allows independent assessment of any disputes arising due to a landlord retaining a deposit for repairs. The landlord must lodge the deposit with an approved scheme or risk a claim from the tenant for compensation.

18.3   VAT

We have discussed the status of new homes for sale for VAT and seen that they are zero-rated. The zero-rated status does not, however, apply to new homes built to rent as rent is exempt from VAT and therefore out of the scope of VAT.

18.4   Management

Residential property management includes all activities required to ensure the smooth operation of let property.

Planned maintenance schedule

A planned maintenance schedule is often prepared by a managing agent. It is a spreadsheet showing all actions required including inspections, surveys and repairs to the building over a twelve month period such that dates are allocated to all necessary actions. Records can then be kept in chronological order with details of the actions taken.

Ground rent

Ground rent is technically the rent paid for the land while the premium is the consideration for the lease itself. This concept has changed in practice over the years as ground rents do not typically reflect the annual value of land and indeed leases that have allowed any contractual mechanism for an increase in ground rents to commercial levels by say, doubling every five years, have been condemned by government. Many developers will have a portfolio of ground rents being the freehold interests of blocks of flats built over years. I became aware of the effect of this once when speaking with a developer who had ground rents from some 200 flats. Surely the management of these blocks did not justify the retention of them as the collection of so many modest ground rents annually was itself a costly exercise let alone the insurance and service charge obligations? The opportunity for forfeiture for non-payment is an unlikely one as there is relief against forfeiture in section 167 of the Commonhold and Leasehold Reform Act 2002 where the ground rent has to have been unpaid for at least three years.

What I had not considered was the effect these freeholds had on this developer's balance sheet. He received some £50,000, which is not a great amount when considering the management issues, but he had found a way of benefitting from this. He capitalised the ground rents at 4%, that is 25 x 50,000 = £1,250,000, a figure that sat very impressively as fixed assets on his balance sheet. This no doubt aided his ability to secure funding and investment.

My own view is that 4% is a very low yield for such an asset but this was at a time when interest rates were particularly low.

18.5   Repairs

With short term lettings of less than seven years there are a number of items, the repair of which falls to the landlord under section 11 Landlord and Tenant Act 1985 (see *Liverpool City Council v Irwin* [1977] A.C. 239).

These are:

• The building's structure and exterior.

• Sanitary fittings including basins, baths, pipes and drains.

- Gas appliances including flues, pipes and ventilation.

- Electrical wiring.

- Consequential damage that occurs from remedial works.

- Communal areas.

The landlord cannot charge the tenant for these repairs.

18.6 Furnished and unfurnished letting
I have found that most tenants require an unfurnished let. There are few who do not have furniture.

18.7 Inventory
The landlord should not overlook the preparation of an inventory of furniture and items within the property, if indeed they are providing them.

18.8 Insurances
Buildings insurance is taken out by the freeholder but is at the cost of the leaseholders under long leases.

18.9 Council tax
The payment of council tax will be the tenant's responsibility where the property is unfurnished and the landlord's responsibility where furnished. This will require the landlord notifying the charging authority of the name of the tenant and the date of occupation.

18.10 Landlord licences
Landlord licences are generally licences issued by local authorities to quali-fying landlords of houses in multiple occupation (HMOs). The licencing of these properties allows the local authority to be assured that the landlord is a responsible one and that the property is suitable for letting as an HMO. Gas certificates, fire certificates and electrical installation certificates will have to be obtained and you would assume that the ownership of the prop-erty would need to be proven. Some local authorities, particularly urban boroughs, have attempted to widen licencing to cover all residential letting. The government has currently restricted this requirement to a maximum of 20% of let property in a borough. Landlords should, however, be sure to check with their borough as it is a criminal offence not to obtain a licence where one is required.

18.11 Services to managed property

Dealing with service companies for various projects in various stages of completion is not the most appealing aspect of property development. The issues for a landlord are the different completion dates of sales and the transfer dates of the services to the buyers. It is possible with a block of flats to limit inspections, visits and arrangements from service companies by centralising the services. Charges are then metered to the tenants who can see from a control panel in the flat the readings for heating and water services. This makes life easier for the tenant who does not have to have any contact with service companies and is able to agree readings for use of services upon departure from the flat.

Chapter 19

Project management for housing associations and custom-build for clients

*'The first step in exceeding your customer's expectations is to
know those expectations.'*
Roy H Williams

I have referred previously to project management as part of the development process. Here the developer steps back from the funding of the project and frees themselves of the risk of an unsold and completed project. They are essentially managing the project for a client and providing they have a client who has the funds to complete the development and the cost of the project is accurately assessed, the developer can be sure that they will make a profit. The risk is thereby reduced but of course the potential reward from the project selling for more than originally estimated is lost to them. My own view is that developers should seek to balance their business models with some speculative projects and some project management. Indeed, I would go as far as to suggest a 50:50 split.

There are two potential clients in the market to have projects managed for them. They are housing associations and custom-build clients.

19.1   Housing associations

Housing associations are private bodies set up to provide housing to low income households. They are registered housing 'providers' funded in part by income from their housing portfolio and partly by the housing corporation (now Homes England).

They hold substantial portfolios of residential property for rent to those who generally require some subsidy to their rent. The largest UK housing association is Clarion with around 125,000 homes let. Other large housing associations include Peabody Trust, Hyde and L&Q but there are many more, some serving specific groups of tenants, some serving specific geographical areas.

Housing associations generally let their homes on assured tenancies but will often carry a portfolio of secured tenancies where they have acquired a portfolio of homes from a local authority. A housing association may have

ASTs in their portfolio and some housing associations will sell homes using profits as 'cross subsidy' for their mainstream activities.

Housing associations are often referred to as Registered Providers (RPs) of housing. This is a reference to the requirement for housing associations to register to qualify for public funding.

Housing associations are often keen to expand their portfolios by acquisition of sites for new build houses and flats. It is perhaps an obvious point but a housing association is unlikely to be interested to buy a site for large detached housing. It is committed to letting smaller houses generally on sites with multiple plots to tenants in housing need.

While some housing associations are content to manage their existing stock, most housing associations will seek to expand their housing stock by building new homes. Few will have their own resources for this but will employ contractors to fulfil this role.

This gives the developer an opportunity to acquire sites for a housing association subject to receiving the construction contract for the homes. Here a developer will have secured a planning permission based on the requirements and specification of affordable homes.

Advantages of housing association contracts
The main advantage of securing a contract with a housing association is that the developer will not have to borrow funds to build out the project. The housing association will provide funds on a monthly basis as approved by a valuation from their employer's agent.

The developer will also not have to sell the properties on completion. They will merely hand them over to the association for them to allocate to their tenants. This removes any uncertainty the developer may have in relation to sales. There are then considerable savings in costs of marketing, estate agents' fees and lawyers' fees, council tax and of course interest that the developer would have had to pay to a funder. Together these costs can, in my experience, add up to a figure similar to any discount sought by the association for taking on the project.

An advantage that I have regard to is the discipline imposed on the development team to stick to the plan. That means sticking to plans and specifications rigorously. It also means sticking to the programme and not letting delays prevent the project achieving target dates.

Disadvantages of housing association contracts

If a developer signs a contract at a price to build a number of homes for a housing association they become the contractor and will therefore not receive any additional consideration if the housing market raises the value of the houses prior to completion. They will have lost that potential profit. The contract with the housing association will be at a fixed price and a fixed programme and therefore the developer will need to be sure of their costs and be ready to commence the project to adhere to the programme.

Housing associations are often seeking 'package deals' where a developer approaches them with a project that they have a contract to buy and have obtained planning permission often with the object of selling the site to a housing association and undertaking the construction of the project for the association. In some circumstances it is possible for the developer to sell the site to the housing association for a small profit to cover the costs incurred in site acquisition and planning and to agree a favourable design build contract.

I can confirm from personal experience that some of my company's more profitable, and indeed enjoyable, projects have been undertaken for housing associations.

Designing homes for housing associations

If it is the intention to sell a project to a housing association, or even if there is the potential possibility that the project may be undertaken for a housing association, it is important that the architect is aware of this so that design and specification meet the criteria of the association. I recall on one occasion having to widen a corridor to meet fire regulations. This reduced one of the flats below the minimum gross internal area required by the association. Fortunately, the planning authority were happy to approve the re-siting of the external wall of the building.

Pre-contract work

The developer may have pre-contract work to carry out prior to construction in the usual way. They will need to ensure that all planning conditions are satisfied and that the building inspector has approved plans. They will need to carry out notifications pursuant to their pre-start meeting, instigate any road or footpath closures and obtain crossover licences where required for the construction process to commence.

The building contract with a housing association

The building contract will usually be signed by the parties on the point of commitment to the purchase of the site, that is to say, a simultaneous exchange of the contracts. The developer will have been responsible for organisation of the design of the project and therefore a design build contract, (JCT DB 2016) will be the appropriate contract to enter into. There will be a number of appendices including contract sum analysis, plans and drawings, build programme and specifications. These will be agreed between the developer and the employer's agent prior to the date of execution of the contract.

It is important to understand the contractual commitments being entered into. I once hired a barrister to talk my team through the contract prior to our entering into it which enabled us to know precisely what to ask the employer's agent and what obligations we had.

19.2   Housing corporation

Registered providers obtain grant funding from what was the housing corporation and now Homes England. This organisation was set up under the Housing Act 1964 to fund affordable housing but it also played a role in the specification of homes it was funding to certain energy standards. This saw housing associations leading the way to more energy efficient new homes with lesser costs of energy for their tenants.

The trend has been for housing associations to grow their portfolios. Often this has been achieved by mergers between associations. This has not been without criticism as some feel that a better service is given to tenants by smaller more local associations. Scale does, however, allow for the increased provision of new homes often built in conjunction with speculative housing by housebuilders for registered providers. This requirement for numbers of homes is relevant to the developer wishing to create a relationship with a housing association as it will quickly be appreciated that few housing associations will be interested in taking on the management of a project with just a small number of units.

19.3   Employer's Agent

The Employer's Agent (EA) is usually a chartered surveyor employed by a firm of construction project managers. Their role is to identify, manage and mitigate risk and check on the quality of the construction to ensure that the housing association's requirements of the project are met. The EA will require site meetings at regular intervals to go through the progress and check the quality and organisation of the works.

19.4   Site staff

It is essential when working with a housing association to understand that the employer's agent will expect to see that a certain discipline is applied on site. Health and safety will be scrutinised including records of attendance on site, induction of operatives and ensuring personal protective clothing is worn. Site management plans for storage, parking and welfare facilities need to be in place. It is generally understood that subcontract labour will be employed on a small housing scheme and I have found that subcontractors like the certainty of a housing association project.

19.5   Project managing for custom-build clients

There are individuals who will wish to buy a plot to have a home built to their own design and specification. We call this approach 'self-build' but in practice many self-builders do not engage in the building work themselves but employ a development manager to oversee the work. The term 'custom-build' is used to describe this approach which I feel better suits the activity.

Custom-build clients will often seek the advice of the development manager not merely on the construction issues but the development and project planning issues as well. The development manager's role then incorporates not just the construction, supervision, procurement, scheduling and budgeting but advice as to planning and related matters. This gives the developer the opportunity to provide a complete service to development manage for custom-build clients.

Development management for custom-build clients is a good way to start a development business that is short of capital or indeed to carry out an additional project within an established business to increase scale. The developer may be carrying out, say, a project of their own but able to development manage a project for a custom-build client at the same time. The advantage will be that the risk of the development project is countered by the cashflow from the client's project while trades can be utilised on both projects. The usual arrangement is for a fee of 5% to 8% of the build cost to be charged for the development management so that while it is not a great profit it is not a great risk. This can be a cost plus contract rather than a fixed price contract which in my view is the better way of navigating the variations of specification, design and programme that are prevalent with custom-build client work.

The National Custom and Self Build Association is a body that recognises the need to involve small developers in the process of assisting custom-build clients. Indeed, its mission is to make custom and self-build a mainstream choice for all those seeking a home of their own. Custom-build is prevalent in many other countries but for some reason has never quite taken off in the UK. The Prime Minister commissioned the Bacon Review to access the opportunities for the growth of 'self-build' housing and this has given the SME developer the opportunity to seek out opportunities for this work.

So, the benefit of project managing or development managing a custom client build for the developer is that the developer does not fund the project. The client is responsible for the funding.

One can imagine, if the developer is fortunate enough to undertake one custom-build client, one housing association project management and one development of their own at the same time, they will create a busy business with its risk and reward spread across three separately funded activities.

The developer need not think that this is unusual. Many listed companies work in this way but on a larger scale, building speculatively while undertaking substantial projects for housing associations and those local authorities who have their own housing portfolios.

Custom-build client work can give great pleasure. I have gained many friends through managing the building of their homes. One has to be aware, however, that this work is extremely time consuming as the client needs to be kept informed every step of the way, and clients do have a habit of specifying fittings that are difficult to source and making variations that cause delays to the programme.

Key skills include general management, troubleshooting, problem solving, quality checking and diplomacy, as well as in-depth knowledge of construction practices and the built environment. The development manager will also oversee and be responsible for health and safety on site.

A development manager will create a programme for the works. They will undertake procurement, calling in quotes from contractors and negotiating the pricing structure, as well as any discounts with suppliers. They will appoint individual contractors, trades, suppliers and services, and decide when each one needs to be on site.

A developer may wish to utilise a custom-build client contract to spread their risk upon a development site that they are acquiring. For example, the acquisition of plots for three detached houses could be undertaken as two for speculative development and one for a custom-build client. In this way part of the site is paid for, part of the cashflow is assured and one of the houses sold. This takes a little more arrangement but it is something I have done on several occasions.

I have found that custom-build client work only seems to pay where good sized detached houses are to be constructed. A small project for a custom-build client simply does not have the capacity to justify the expense of a development manager. However, if the custom-build client contract is one house within a larger development it may contribute more than just the spread of risk by the economies of scale the additional house brings to the development. It thereby makes the contract worthwhile.

There are a number of considerations the developer should take into account with custom-build client work. First, it is as well to be sure that the client has not underestimated the cost of the project. A realistic contract sum analysis should be discussed early on in the project. Variations are almost inevitable in custom-build client work and it is often the case that clients will be aware of the cost of the variation but be unaware of the additional cost of the disruption and delay caused by that variation.

Design and specification can often be too ambitious and the development manager should consider carefully any contract that seeks innovative design and specification of materials that are difficult to source.

Custom-build clients are often unaware of requirements such as insurance, new homes warranties, building inspection, health and safety inspection and site accommodation. While these always come at a cost they are often overlooked by the client in their budget.

The best custom-build client job I undertook was for a client who signed the contract and declared that he was flying to Borneo the following day and that he would be away for a year. He had seen an identical house I had built so was happy with the style and specification. 'I shall just leave it to you,' he said. On his return he was delighted to move in to a completed house following a trip on which he commented, 'I knew I was a long way from home when I saw I was the only person on the plane wearing shoes.'

In summary then, I am always pleased to take on a custom client project that is well funded and gives monthly cashflow, where I can settle subcontractor invoices on behalf of the client, where there are few variations and clear specification and where design is uncomplicated. Such a project can be of great benefit to the development company.

Case study 11
Project management for custom-build client.
Key issue: Whether the project would contribute to the developer's cashflow or require too much time for it to be worthwhile.

The client had approached the developer to submit a price to build a substantial detached house in a prestige area. The contract sum would be substantial and could therefore contribute to the developer's cashflow in a positive way. It was to be a construction project, the planning design and project planning having been done by professional consultants.

The key issue is to look at the requirements of the proposed contract and the potential liability of that contract plus the design and specification of the house and the timescale involved in its construction.

First then – the contract. The developer will wish to ensure that there is profit in the work and that they are taking on responsibility for construction work that they are capable of completing. Often the client's requirements are very different from the design and specification of a house built speculatively. This has an important impact on the pricing and sourcing of labour and materials. A fixed price contract might not be the best way to proceed under such circumstances. Perhaps a cost plus percentage or fee contract would work better where the developer is guaranteed a profit and where speculation is taken out.

The programme can become extended in two ways. First, the client can spend a great deal of time making choices of specification and variations and secondly, they may simply not have the funds to fulfil their ambitious project. The developer must be aware of the potential for delays and reach an agreement as to how they may be dealt with. Disruption in a build programme will incur cost and there should be a mechanism for calculating this.

Summary of the proposed contract
Notwithstanding the cashflow advantage of taking on this contract, the design and specification that are considered may be too specialist. In this case the contract was fixed price and the developer could not risk the impact on the costs that may occur. The decision was taken to decline to take the contract.

Chapter 20

Disputes between parties in development and construction

'Litigation is a machine you go into as a pig and come out as a sausage.'
Ambrose Bierce

It is an unfortunate aspect of the activities of construction and development that they engender expectations that are sometimes unfulfilled by outcomes. Misunderstandings can arise from failure to read plans and specifications or to appreciate the consequences of decisions as to matters such as materials and design. They are thereby activities that provide the potential for disputes.

Disputes can be reconciled between the parties by compromise but occasionally one party insists on their position and the dispute becomes not only costly where there is the engagement of lawyers and professional advisors, but takes up the developer's time which is better spent on more productive activities.

Here I consider some of the kinds of disputes that the developer might encounter and the remedies and processes in their avoidance and resolution.

20.1   Developer disputes with buyers

Where a developer sells a residential property they generally do so with a new home warranty such that any significant claim for financial loss due to structural failure is covered on an insurance basis. We have already seen that the sale of land is subject to the caveat emptor rule and thereby, subject to the developer not having misrepresented the property sold, they are not liable in contract. We have seen too that pure economic loss is not recoverable from the developer in tort. Where injury or death occurs as a result of the negligence of members of a development team this will no doubt involve a developer, but this is something outside the scope of this heading. The usual position is that, other than remedial snagging, the developer who has sold the property to the buyer is not liable for defects that are pure economic loss unless the sale contract has been written in a way that extends liability.

20.2   Developer disputes with contractors

Disputes do sometimes arise between developers and main contractors and usually there will be a claim for damages either from the developer against the main contractor for faulty workmanship or liquidated damages for delay in completion, or from the contractor against the developer for non-payment by the developer.

When disputes arise the question first asked is, 'What is in the contract?'

A construction contract should always be subject to dispute resolution by adjudication. It may contain a clause requiring mediation or arbitration as a means of resolving any dispute. This will mean that many issues will be resolved without the necessity of going to court.

20.3   Litigation

Litigation in construction and development disputes involves the process of legal action in a civil court, generally to secure damages for some form of financial loss. The parties to the action are therefore the claimant and the defendant. The process is time consuming and expensive and indeed it can take a considerable time for a case to come to court. The developer will be well advised to avoid litigation if at all possible.

It seems to me that litigation often tends to steer away from the issue that was first identified and focus on some obscure legal uncertainty. The case thus goes forward with the mission of solving a technical legal question rather than the dispute itself.

The kinds of disputes that can arise in development and construction are most often claims for financial damages for breach of contract. Such claims invariably involve expensive expert witnesses to give evidence on behalf of the parties or expertise to the court on technical matters.

There is always good reason to avoid expensive and time-consuming litigation.

20.4   Mediation

Mediation is a process where parties meet with a mutually selected impartial person who assists in negotiating a solution to their dispute.

It is an alternative to litigation which tends to be swifter and more relevant to construction issues, particularly where a professional surveyor with experience in construction matters acts as mediator.

A construction contract will often incorporate a clause where a mediation process of some kind should be used prior to any court action.

20.5   Arbitration

Where litigation is brought to court the outcome can become publicised. Many litigants wish to avoid this and prefer arbitration as it is a private procedure governed under the Arbitration Act 1996. For this reason, the process is paid for by the parties in equal amounts although the arbitrator has the power to order costs. Indeed, many contracts encountered in construction and development contain an arbitration clause that states that disputes should be referred to arbitration. There are several benefits to arbitration. The arbitrator is often a chartered surveyor or architect who is experienced in construction matters. They will act as judge and jury and the arbitration award, or decision they make, is final save in very exceptional circumstances. Often arbitration is quicker than litigation and less expensive.

20.6   Adjudication

There is statutory right in section 108 Construction Act 1996 for either party to a construction contract to refer a dispute in any construction contract to a construction adjudicator without any need for that right to be expressed in the contract. Adjudication is therefore the most common method of alternative dispute resolution and courts recommend its use as part of a pre-action protocol. The process takes 28 days and the adjudicator is usually a chartered quantity surveyor.

Where a contractor enters a building contract to construct a building for a client as opposed to a buyer, the client becomes the employer under the contract. They can claim against the main contractor for financial damages occasioned by act or omission by the contractor or indeed their subcontractor. This is because there is privity of contract and the construction contract is not for the sale of land and thereby not subject to the caveat emptor rule.

A claim made by the employer directly of a subcontractor generally will require that a collateral contract has been entered into by the subcontractor for the benefit of the employer.

There is generally no assumption of responsibility by the subcontractor direct to the employer, the parties having so structured their relationship that it is inconsistent with any such assumption of responsibility (see Lord Goff in *Henderson v Merrett Syndicates* [1994] UKHL 5).

There are exceptions to this rule. If the subcontractor owed a duty of care to the employer then a relationship may have arisen whereby the tort of negligence can be the basis of claim.

20.7   Developer land disputes

Disputes in relation to land might relate to the contract of purchase where a vendor has misrepresented their property or there is ambiguity as to certain arrangements. They may relate to boundaries where neighbours, often conscious of development proposals, seek to establish adverse possession of areas that they have encroached upon. Disputes may relate to third party rights such as easements or restrictive covenants or they may relate to planning matters. Many land related disputes can be referred to the First-tier Tribunal (Property Chamber) which is the specialist tribunal for property related matters.

20.8   Contract disputes

In English law of contract the starting point is that parties to that contract enter it freely and courts are often reluctant to revise or amend terms of a contract between parties. Uncertainty as to terms can often result in disputes, however, and oppressive clauses can be questioned on an equitable basis.

20.9   Statutory demands

A statutory demand is a first step for a creditor seeking to bankrupt the debtor due to non-payment of a debt. It is often a scare tactic to bring the debtor to the negotiating table. Securing the debtor's bankruptcy will probably not do the creditor much good in practical terms of obtaining payment especially if they have no assets. It is important, however, for the debtor to react to a statutory demand and understand that they must submit an Insolvency Act Application Notice, Form IAA Rule 135, to the court named on the demand within 18 days of receipt of the statutory demand or risk the creditor taking action for bankruptcy. If there is a dispute regarding the statutory demand then it may be set aside by the court.

20.10   Courts and tribunals
Small claims court

Civil action for the recovery of money takes place in the small claims court or, for greater sums, the county court.

The small claims court deals with private disputes that do not involve a large sum of money. Typically, then, a claim may be made by a subcontractor for a retention being held by a main contractor where remedial work has been undertaken and the quantum of the retention is thereby disputed.

County court

County courts are the principal courts for civil actions. They are located throughout the country and each hearing is presided over by a single judge. In debt cases the aim of a claimant taking county court action against a defendant is to secure a county court judgement. This is a legal order to pay the whole amount of the debt. Judgements can be enforced at the request of the claimant by bailiffs seizing a defendant's property or an order of attachment to earnings can be made.

Technology and Construction Court

This court is part of the High Court in London. It handles disputes about buildings, engineering and surveying and claims relating to services of construction professionals, claims about local authority duties relating to land and buildings and challenges to arbitration awards.

Residential property tribunals

First-tier Tribunal (Property Chamber)

The First-tier Tribunal handles disputes including leasehold matters such as rent increases, enfranchisement and land registration matters for residential property. A panel of three people oversees cases brought before the tribunal (generally consisting of a solicitor, a chartered surveyor and one other expert). It is located at Alfred Place in London and other locations around the country.

Upper Tribunal Lands Chamber

The Upper Tribunal handles appeals from the First-tier Tribunal, Leasehold Valuation Tribunals and Valuation Tribunals. The Lands Chamber is one of the four chambers within the Upper Tribunal that has taken on the functions of the Lands Tribunal. It has the status of a High Court and it deals with matters of compulsory purchase, restrictive covenants, rates and taxes and tree preservation orders. The tribunal sits at Fetter Lane in London.

20.11 Summary

In my experience developers are not the most adept of parties to legal disputes. Developers tend to be optimistic as to the outcome of any relationship. They tend to be willing to reach a compromise and poor at keeping those written records that are often so vital in the determination of a dispute. In addition there is always the next deal to devote time to. The best advice is therefore to avoid disputes wherever possible.

Conclusion

I hope that this book has helped as a guide through the development process and provided answers to some of the questions that frequently arise while undertaking a development project. This subject is however far too fulsome to be the subject of just one book and the reader may well wish to read more on the subjects I have referred to. The reader may wish to look deeper into the subject and read some of these.

Further reading

Branson, Richard	Losing My Virginity	Virgin Publishing
Carpenter & Harris	Property Auctions	Estates Gazette
Chappell, David	The JCT Design and Build Contract	Blackwell Publishing
Chudley & Greeno	Building Construction Handbook	Butterworths
Crosby & Wyatt	Valuation of Development Property	RICS
De Soto, Hernando	The Mystery of Capital	Bantum Press
Franks, James	Building Contract Administration and Practice	Batsford
Gaunt & Morgan	Gale on Easements	Sweet & Maxwell
Harvey & Ashworth	The Construction Industry of Great Britain	Butterworths
Harvey-Jones, John	Making it Happen	HarperCollins
Goodall, Martin	The Use of Land and Buildings	Bath Publishing
Graham, Tom	The Environment Act 2021	Bath Publishing
Gray, Kevin & Susan	Elements of Land Law	Butterworths
Marriott, Oliver	The Property Boom	Abingdon
Megarry & Wade	The Law of Real Property	Sweet & Maxwell
Bowes, Ashley	A Practical Approach to Planning Law	Oxford
Morrow, Nicol Stuart	Party Walls: A Practical Guide	RIBA Publishing
Prebble, John	The Highland Clearances	Penguin
Preston & Newsom	Restrictive Covenants Affecting Freehold Land	Sweet & Maxwell
Pugh-Smith, John	Neighbours and the Law	Sweet & Maxwell
Sara, Colin	Boundaries & Easements	Sweet & Maxwell
Tucker, Benjamin	What is Property?	Whitlock
Zutshi, Simon	Property Magic	Panoma Press

Statute law

Statute law is that law set out by statute (Acts of Parliament). Common law is that derived from judge-made decisions or precedents. English law derives from both sources.

I list more commonly encountered statutes and some precedents (legal cases) that deal with issues often encountered in development together with a note of the subject matter of the case. The reader may wish to research further with a legal textbook, copy of the Act or case summary.

Below is a list of Acts of Parliament most often encountered in Projects in Property:

Arbitration Act 1986
Regulates arbitration proceedings in England and Wales.

Agricultural Holdings Act 1948
Agricultural tenancies. Statutory succession rights.

Agricultural Holdings Act 1986
Agricultural tenancies. Lifetime security of tenure.

Auctions (Bidding Agreements) Act 1969
Prevention of illegal bidding practices.

Building Act 1984
Establishment of building regulations.

Commons Registration Act 1965
Protection of greens and common land in towns and villages.

Commonhold and Leasehold Reform Act 2002
Section 166 notices. Section 167 relief against forfeiture.

Control of Pollution Act 1974
Licensing and disposal of controlled waste.

Electricity Act 1989
Powers and duties of electricity providers 'licence holders'.

Employment Rights Act 1996
Employment of subcontractors.

Estate Agents Act 1979
Regulates the duties and obligations of estate agents.

Environment Act 1995
Establishment of the Environment Agency.

Environment Act 2021
Biodiversity.

Environmental Protection Act 1990
Integrated pollution protection and control (IPPC).

Finance Act 2015
Reduced allowance of costs against rental income.

Gas Act 1986
Powers of gas transporters.

Health and Safety at Work etc. Act 1974
Requirements for health and safety of employees.

Highways Act 1980
Adoption of new estate roads (section 38).

Housing Act 1988
Assured and assured shorthold tenancies.

Land Charges Act 1972
Registration of charges over unregistered land.

Landlord and Tenant Act 1927
Tenants' improvement compensation. Business tenancies.

Landlord and Tenant Act 1954
Business tenancies security of tenure Part 2.

Landlord and Tenant (Covenants) Act 1995
Release of covenants on assignment of tenancy or reversion.

Land Registration Act 1925
Introduction of land registration.

Land Registration Act 1988
Amendments to the 1925 Act.

Land Registration Act 2002
Amendments to the 1925 Act.

Land Powers (Defence) Act 1958
Limitation on building work by pipelines. Section 16.

Law of Property Act 1925
Significant consolidation of property law.

Law of Property Act 1969
Amends Part II of the Landlord and Tenant Act 1954.

Leasehold Reform Act 1967
Enfranchisement rights to leaseholders.

Local Government Act 1972
Creation of Metropolitan and non-Metropolitan county and district councils.

Local Government (Miscellaneous Provisions) Act 1982
Enforceability of covenants without time limit (section 33).

Local Government and Housing Act 1989
Security of tenure on ending of long residential tenancies.

Rent Act 1977
Regulated tenancies.

Planning and Compensation Act 1991
Extension of powers to acquire land and to give compensation.

Planning (Listed Buildings and Conservation Areas) Act 1990
Changed law relating to planning for listed buildings.

Protection from Eviction Act 1977
Protection of residential tenants from harassment and illegal eviction.

Party Wall etc. Act 1996

Regulates construction work to avoid damage to neighbouring property.

Pipe-Lines Act 1962

Compulsory acquisition of rights to install a pipeline. Cessation of use section 36.

New Roads and Street Works Act 1991

Licences to work in public highway (section 50).

Town and Country Planning Act 1990

Planning requirements. Development section 55. Commencement of development. Section 56 planning obligations. Section 106.

Water Industry Act 1991

Powers of water and sewerage undertakers. Agreements to connect to public sewers. Section 106.

Water Resources Act 1991

Powers of Environment Agency.

Case law

Here is a list of legal cases that may be of interest to the developer of Projects in Property.

Allen & Others v Veranne Builders (1988) NPC 11
Building scheme of restrictive covenants.

Associated Provincial Picture Houses v Wednesbury Corporation [1948] 1 K.B. 223
Wednesbury rules. The test of reasonableness exercised by a planning authority.

Attwood v Bovis Homes [2001] Ch 379; All ER 948
Change in use of easement did not render it void.

Breskar v Wall [1971] 126 C.L.R. 376
Title by registration.

Currie v Misa (1875) LR 10 Ex 153
Definition of consideration.

Dyce v Lady Jane Hay (1852) 1 Macq 305
Servitudes and easements must alter and expand with the changes that take place in the circumstances of mankind.

Ellison v Reacher (1908) 2 Ch 374
Four points that are the basis of a building scheme of covenants.

Estate Governors of Alleyn's College of God's Gift at Dulwich v Williams [1994] 23 E.G. 127
Leasehold Reform Act 1967. Scheme of management.

Federated Homes Ltd v Mill Lodge Properties Ltd [1980] 1 W.L.R. 594
Section 78 Law of Property Act 1925. Restrictive covenant attaches to every part of land.

FG Whitley and Sons v SoS for Wales [1990] J.P.L. 675
Operation in breach of a condition cannot start a development.

Graham v Philcox [1984] Q.B. 747
Easement granted to tenant attached to freehold.

Hair v Gilman (2000) 80 P. & C.R. 108
Right to park a car can be an easement.

Hanily v Minister of Local Government and Planning [1952] 1 All E.R. 129
Anyone who properly hoped to acquire an interest in the land could apply for planning permission.

Henderson v Merrett Syndicates [1994] UKHL 5
Duty of care in tort can exist in addition to contract.

Hibbitt v SSCLG [2016] EWHC 2853 (Admin)
Permitted development has to be conversion not rebuild.

High Peak BC v SSE [1981] J.P.L. 366
Legal start of development by digging trench.

Jelbert v Davis [1968] 1 W.L.R. 589
Injunction may be granted to restrain excessive use of an easement.

Liverpool City Council v Irwin [1977] A.C. 239
Landlord responsible for essential parts of block of flats.

Martin v Lipton [2020] UKUT 8 (LC)
Modification of restrictive covenant.

Murphy v Brentwood DC [[1991] 1 A.C. 398
House of Lords decision on pure economic loss.

Newbury DC v SSE [1981] A.C. 578
Three tests re planning conditions (*Newbury* rules).

Parkhurst Road Ltd v SSLG & Anor [2018] EWHC 991 (Admin)
Provision of affordable housing in accordance with plan policies.

Pimlico Plumbers Ltd v Smith [2018] UKSC 29
Employment rights.

Pritchard v Briggs [1980] Ch 338
Registered option to purchase land takes precedence over prior rights of pre-emption.

Re Ellenborough Park (1956) Ch 131
The four characteristics of an easement.

R v Hillingdon LBC Ex p Royco Homes Ltd [1974] 1 Q.B. 720
Statutory powers can only be exercised for the purpose for which it is given.

Rylands v Fletcher (1868) LR 3 HL 330
Strict liability in negligence.

Shropshire Council v SSCLG [2019] EWHC 16 (Admin)
CIL payments.

Stokes v Cambridge Corporation (1961) 13 P. & C.R. 77
Valuation of access land.

Street v Mountford [1985] A.C. 809
Distinction between a lease and a licence

Stringer v Minister of Housing and Local Government [1970] 1 W.L.R. 128
Any consideration which relates to the use and development of the land is capable of being a planning consideration.

Wheeldon v Burrows (1879) 12 Ch D 31
Implied easements.

Yeoman's Row Management Ltd & Anor v Cobbe [2008] UKHL 55
Contracts for the sale and purchase of land must be in writing.

Appendices

Pre-contract site report

The pre-contract report is the collation of all the matters that have been researched prior to the purchase contract being exchanged i.e. a kind of checklist. Increasingly this is referred to as 'due diligence', a term that derives from company acquisitions.

The developer is encouraged to record all information about the project however irrelevant this may appear. The pre-contract report thereby becomes a useful source of reference when the project is proceeding.

Plot X dated 20/08/2023

General description
The site is an irregular shape lying in a valley just south east of Y village which includes a mill pond and river frontage to the east. The buildings on the site have been used by Z animal feed merchants.

There is an existing water mill which is listed grade 2 and will be retained as part of the scheme. The other buildings are all to be demolished.

Area
3.2 acres.

Levels
A full land survey has been undertaken by [****] survey and this has formed the basis for the planning application.

Levels have been forwarded to the consultant [****].

Existing buildings
The listed water mill is to be retained as part of the scheme.

There are four further buildings which have been used for storage and manufacture of animal feed and which are to be demolished.

No structural survey has been undertaken of the listed building but it has been examined by RDP and a substantial allowance made for its refurbishment.

Insurance of this building will be implemented on legal completion of the purchase.

Surrounding buildings
There are just two buildings in the grounds around the site. Both are low rise residential. These buildings are not listed and both seem to have been associated with activities of the water mill in the past.

Rights of light and party walls are not issues to be concerned with.

Care needs to be taken with delineation of the boundary between the site and the Mill House which is not clear on the ground.

We may need to pick up land drains from neighbouring property.

Access
[****] is an adopted highway. Access is along a private drive owned by the site. Sight lines to the highway are well established. There is a strip of land between the highway and the access. Access rights across this strip are well established but easements for services are unclear. It is proposed that a strip of land to the side of the access be transferred as part of the purchase so that services can be laid without disturbing the road.

There is no need to widen the access.

Planning
Planning permission 18/123456/FULL 15/04/2018 expired on 15/04/2021.

Conditions attached to this permission were:

(1)   Phasing plan of works to be undertaken.

(2)   Boundary treatments.

(3)   Detailed remediation scheme. This has now been carried out.

(4)   Remediation scheme. This pre-commencement condition will require a verification report upon its completion.

(5)   Details of a clear span bridge. The fresh application seeks to avoid this condition.

(6) Surface water drainage system. This will be taken into account within the hydrology scheme and in consultation with [****] engineers.

(7) Brickwork sample panel constructed on site.

(8) Tile samples.

(9) Sections of drawings.

Listed building consent 18/123456/ABC 04/12/2018 was granted in respect of the listed mill.

A fresh planning application has been submitted 08/01/2023 for the company's scheme following a pre-application meeting and response dated 30/07/2022.

It is not envisaged that there will be a requirement for section 106 or CIL contributions. It is, however, anticipated that the fresh planning permission will recite the above conditions.

A full tree survey has been submitted with the application.

Scheme
The scheme is for retention of the listed mill and conversion of this building into a single house, 3 new terraced houses and two further detached houses with garages and parking. The estate road will be largely as it exists.

Local authority: ABC Borough Council, Planning Services, Town Hall, 1 High Street, Toytown tel. 01234 567891

Planning officer: AN Other.

Consultants: a team list is attached showing the consultants working on the Scheme.

Legal
Titles for the land are: K12345, K98765, K24680 and TT4567.

These have been checked against the survey drawing.

Restrictive covenants
There are reciprocal covenants in the 20/03/2021 transfer of The Bungalow relating to maintenance obligations. There is nothing to restrict development.

Easements
The driveway is subject to rights of way in favour of the two houses to the west of the site. There is a public footpath crossing the site utilising the existing tarmacked area.

There is a legal easement for a land drain across part of the site to the river. It is not clear whether this runs in any recognised channel.

Fresh easements will be taken across the access where it joins BCD Hill pursuant to a statutory declaration 28/02/2020 and an indemnity insurance will be obtained in respect of implied easements over the small area of land between the building to the east and the site.

Adverse occupation
The occupation of the site includes a small area of unregistered land between the building to the east and the main body of the site. This is clearly in use by the site owners. It is proposed that a defective title insurance be taken out on completion to cover this and a quotation has been received.

There is no encroachment from adjoining land upon inspection.

Contract
JKL Ltd 13579, an SPV company, will be exchanging a contract conditional upon the grant of fresh planning permission. The anticipated date for exchange of this conditional contract is 14/06/2023. The contract will be made unconditional upon grant of planning permission and legal completion will be within 28 days thereafter.

Drainage
Existing
Foul: There is a rising main to a manhole within the access drive.

Surface: Surface water drains to the river.

Proposed
It is proposed that use is made of the existing sewer which will by common residential use become a lateral drain.

Surface water will drain to the river.

Sluice
The sluice has been opened up and is functioning as part of the mill pond system together with a spillway and culvert.

Ground conditions
Soil report
A full Part 2 report has been undertaken by FGH environmental surveyors.

Foundations envisaged
Subsoil is desiccated in some areas and it is clear that short bored piling will need to be used.

Build costs and abnormal costs
A viability is attached showing build cost for the new houses at £155.00 per ft² for the new houses and £250.00 per ft² for the conversion.

Abnormals
(1)   Cost of converting the mill building including compliance with heritage requirements and architects' work.

(2)   Implementation of the hydrology requirements including excavation of the pond, banking of the pond works to the culverts and sluice system.

(3)   Remediation scheme, excavation, cart away, importation of clean soil.

(4)   Short bored piling.

(5)   Demolition of existing buildings.

Sales
A sales survey has been conducted with PQR estate agents.

Plot	ft² GIA	Sale price
Plot 1: End terrace 3-bed	1,154 ft²	£580,000
Plot 2: Mid terrace 3-bed	1,154 ft²	£570,000
Plot 3: End terrace 3-bed	1,154 ft²	£595,000

Plot 4: Detached 5-bed paddock	3,437 ft²	£1,550,000
Plot 5: Detached 4-bed	2,728 ft²	£1,325,000
Plot 6: Detached 3-bed existing unit	2,898 ft²	£1,250,000
Total		£5,870,000

Viability
A full viability is attached.

Results and conclusions
The planning application is submitted. The hydrology has to be approved by the Environment Agency.

A heads of terms has been agreed and forwarded to lawyers.

Attachments
- Location plans and maps
- Team list
- Viability
- Planning permission
- Tree report
- Ecology report
- Hydrology report
- DTI insurance quotation

Action
Environmental
We need to establish whether PAH is classed as hazardous. If it is, it needs to be carted away. If not, it can be used on site. The requirement is to scrape 600mm from the gardens and replace with clean topsoil. We therefore need to dimension the garden areas and get some idea of costing. My understanding is that PAH is indeed non-hazardous waste.

We need a quote from the demolition contractor to cart away the hazardous waste. My understanding is that this will be just north of £30,000.

Naming
It would be useful to establish a postal address for the site as the lane is unnamed. Mill Lane seems the obvious choice or possibly Watermill Lane.

I will attend to that.

Demolition
We should appoint a demolition contractor as soon as possible.

Groundworker
As soon as PMS confirm foundations we should appoint our groundworker.

We will then have about 10 weeks to organise following trades.

Please note that I would like to deepen the pond by about a metre depositing the arising by the northern bank to enlarge the garden by the old mill. My intention is that the pond will be a permanent feature.

Consultants
Please find team list attached.

Working drawings
We have instructed [****] to move ahead with the working drawings for the terraced houses which are to be timber frame and the existing mill building which will no doubt require a great many sections and detailed drawing work.

We intend to tender the terrace for timber frame quotes as soon as possible.

Construction method statement
There is no requirement for a construction method statement but I think that we should prepare something given the existing footpath access deliveries and cart away especially.

Services
I intend to obtain confirmation of availability of services so that the M&E consultant can follow up with quotations, works and timescales.

Pond
I think we all will need to understand how the sluice and spillway work. I will make arrangements for some instruction.

Agenda for the pre-build meeting

The pre-build meeting should take place prior to commencement of construction work. It is useful to identify site arrangements, storage, access, welfare and parking, methods of construction, health and safety and notifications of commencement to neighbours.

Site: [••••]

Surveyor: [••••]

Site manager: [••••]

Project manager: [••••]

Date: [••••]

Review drawings
Check they are the latest drawings against drawing issue sheet.

Identify any potential health and safety risks
Eliminate where possible and provide method statements where necessary.

Review what building regulations remain to be satisfied
Ensure that the building inspector has been appointed for the project and ensure that they are supplied with drawings.

Clarify new homes warranty. Premium. Cover. Surveyor.

Review planning conditions
Identify any outstanding conditions. Note compliance conditions and ensure these are recorded on site, e.g. tree protection.

Review subcontractor procurement schedule
Ensure that all trades are listed. Agree who appoints. Agree any nominated subcontractors.

Programme and personnel
Discuss programme. Evaluate peak personnel numbers on site and ensure no conflicting activities.

Parking and turning

Consider parking for site personnel and turning and unloading of deliveries.

Review legal requirements

Footpath and road closures. Highway operations. Contract conditions.

Health and safety and risk assessment

Complete F10 online. Identify risks.

Letter of engagement

This is the letter engaging the professionals in the project. It should describe the role required of the professional in the project and seek confirmation of the appointment in writing. It is useful in this letter to confirm the requirement for a collateral warranty to the funder whether or not this will be required, together with a copy of the Professional Indemnity insurance. Funders will often insist on seeing this letter to be satisfied of the veracity of the engagement.

ABC Associates
2 High Street
Toytown

20/08/2023

Re: Phase 2, 4 High Street, Toytown
Four detached houses. Structural drawings and calculations

I am pleased to confirm that XYZ has completed its purchase of the four plots that are to make up phase 2 of this development. Work is due to commence on 1/10/23. Accordingly, I would be pleased if you will provide a quotation for structural engineers' drawings for the project. I enclose a site plan and working drawings prepared by the architect.

The construction of these houses will be masonry as shown on the drawings with factory made roof trusses.

I attach a soils report prepared by Soils Ltd who propose that the foundations be short bored piles to a depth of 6 metres.

We will enter into a JCT design build contract and will require a collateral warranty from you in favour of our funder.

We also will require a copy of your PI insurance policy.

I look forward to hearing from you.

Yours sincerely,

AN Other

Viability

This important document will be submitted to a funder to establish the figures required for approval of finance. It will also 'firm up' the residual valuation and should therefore be prepared ahead of any contractual commitment. The format of a development viability might be the developer's own but there are many examples in use by valuers and developers that can be purchased from various sources.

4 High Street, Toytown. Date: 20/08/2023			
GDV		**£**	**£**
Anticipated sales price		2,670,000	
Total GDV			2,670,000
Sales costs		45,050	
Net development value			**2,624,950**
Expenditure			
Construction – build costs		1,053,360	
Construction – roads and sewers		11,000	
Construction – overheads		60,000	
Construction – contingency		50,000	
Construction – fees		47,000	
			1,221,360
Finance costs			
Bank fees		50,463	
Bank interest		107,116	
Shareholder interest		0	
Total finance		157,579	157,579
Site acquisition	27%	720,900	720,900
Total costs			2,099,836
Profit	20%		525,114

Sales survey

The sales survey is merely a spreadsheet listing the flats or houses to be built in the project in a column on the left with further columns for values headed with the name of the estate agent giving their opinion. These figures will give the developer the information needed for the initial residual valuation of the site.

Sales survey Date 20/08/2023						
4 High Street, Toytown						
Estate agent	Green	Black	Brown	Red	White	Average
Plot 1	450,000	475,000	450,000	475,000	450,000	460,000
Plot 2	475,000	475,000	475,000	475,000	450,000	470,000
Plot 3	500,000	495,000	500,000	500,000	475,000	494,000
Plot 4	375,000	395,000	395,000	375,000	350,000	378,000
Plot 5	350,000	375,000	350,000	375,000	350,000	360,000
Estimated GDV	2,150,000	2,215,000	2,170,000	2,200,000	2,075,000	2,162,000

Letter inviting tender

This is a letter to be sent to subcontractors inviting their tenders.

The letter should set out the schedule of works and be sure to include everything. Any items missed out will be sure to attract additional variation costs. It is usual to seek at least three tenders for each work package and I know surveyors who will seek five. I have often found quotations to be very different in pricing, generally dependant on the forward order book of the subcontractor.

ABC
Drylining contractor
10 High Street
Toytown

20/08/2023

Dear ABC

Re: Phase 2, 4 High Street, Toytown
Drylining contract for four new timber frame houses

I write to invite your tender for the above described site which is shown on the attached location plan outlined in red.

The plans and drawings are attached as follows.

House type A, plots 1 and 3: Floor plans and elevations

House type B, plots 2 and 4: Floor plans and elevations

The company operates a logistics plan for its sites to include the following:

- Health and safety plan

- Subcontractor induction

- Site rules and risk assessment

- Protective clothing

Parking on site is organised for trades. Hours of work are 08.00 to 16.00 weekdays; 08.00 to 12.00 Saturdays.

We anticipate that the timescale for the drylining works will be 4 months from the date of this letter.

Schedule of works
(1)   Provide all thermal, acoustic and fire insulation to internal walls and ceilings as shown on drawings. External walls will be insulated by timber frame contractor.

(2)   Supply and lay floor screed to ground floor.

(3)   Supply and fit 18mm drylining to all walls and ceilings.

(4)   Supply and apply render to gables on plots 2 and 4 as shown on drawings.

Should you wish to visit the site you may contact our site manager Bill Smith on 01234 678889.

We look forward to receiving your tender.

AN Other

Site safety rules and site induction form

The contractor should write a set of site safety rules on a single sheet of paper and display this in a prominent position on site. The form should be signed by subcontractors confirming induction to the site rules. Signed copies should be kept in the health and safety documents on site.

List of rules for this project

(1) No person will be allowed on site if it is believed that they are under the influence of alcohol or drugs.

(2) Only authorised Licensed Asbestos Contractors to carry out work on asbestos.

(3) Works generating significant noise only to be undertaken during designated hours.

(4) Smoking is only allowed in designated areas.

(5) No radios or personal hifi are allowed in work areas.

(6) Horse play in any form will not be tolerated on site.

(7) All PPE as indicated by the Site Manager is to be used correctly.

(8) Work areas must be kept clean and tidy at all times to minimise trip hazards.

(9) Operatives may only operate plant and equipment for which they are authorised.

(10) All portable electrical equipment used on site will be either battery operated or 110 volt.

(11) Any hazards encountered should be brought to the attention of the Site Manager.

(12) Health and safety and welfare facilities must not be abused.

(13) All visitors to site must report to the site office. It should be noted that only visitors with appropriate PPE will be permitted on to site.

(14) Safe systems of work must be observed at all times.

(15) Site personnel must use only designated access and egress routes.

(16) Care must be taken not to create hazards when storing material on site.

(17) Waste and arisings will only be disposed of in accordance with the official agreed procedure, no dumping of waste or tipping of liquids into drains will be allowed.

(18) All persons are asked to cooperate in creating a safe site. Those that do not may be asked to be excluded from this project and any future projects.

It is useful to have operatives inducted and asked to sign a copy of the site rules.

Induction to site
Site rules and site procedures before work starts.
AT: 4 High Street, Toytown

Site Manager: AN Other

(1) I have provided details of trade qualifications/experience.

(2) I have understood the Method Statements for the tasks I am to perform. I have been trained in the use of the equipment I will be using.

(3) I have PPE and agree that I must wear it on site.

(4) I understand the emergency procedures: evacuation route, closest medical facility, emergency services contacts and communications.

(5) I know where the first aid is kept. I know who the first aiders are. I know who will inform the Site Manager if first aid needs replacement. I know who to contact as a health and safety representative.

(6) I know where the fire extinguishers are.

(7) I know where the toilets and canteen are.

(8) I know the procedures for reporting accidents.

(9) I know the site security measures.

(10) I am medically fit to undertake the tasks I am contracted to do.

(11) I am legally entitled to work in the United Kingdom.

(12) I have received induction to the site from the Site Manager.

Name

Signature

Date

Contractor.

Variations order

This is a simple document I like to attach to the building contract. All variations should be recorded and signed for by the site manager. The document can be hand-written and filed on site under each separate trade. Payment should only be made for variations recorded in this way.

Site: 4 High Street, Toytown

Date: 27 January 2023

Subcontractor: ABC carpentry

Rep: AN Other

Explanation
Day works for additional studwork.

Cost: 5 x days at £240.00 = £1,200.00

Agreed by: Bob Builder

Status: Site manager

Date: 28 January 2023

Index

E

F

M

N

W·